P9-CRP-532

THE HANDBOOK OF PSYCHOLOGY

Drew Appleby
Marian College

 LONGMAN

An imprint of Addison Wesley Longman, Inc.

New York • Reading, Massachusetts • Menlo Park, California • Harlow, England
Don Mills, Ontario • Sydney • Mexico City • Madrid • Amsterdam

The Handbook of Psychology by Drew Appleby

Copyright © 1997 Longman Publishers USA, a division of Addison Wesley Longman, Inc.

All rights reserved. No part of this book may be reproduced, stored in a retrieval system, or transmitted in any form or by any means electronic, mechanical, photocopying, recording, or otherwise, without the prior permission of the publisher.

ISBN: 0-673-98455-9

97 98 99 00 01 9 8 7 6 5 4 3 2 1

This book is dedicated to the thousands of Marian College students I have taught during my quarter century as a teacher of psychology. The pleasure I have derived from watching them develop from uncertain freshman to confident seniors and, in some cases, to professional colleagues is the greatest reward I could ever hope to receive.

CONTENTS

PREFACE

I wrote this book to help you understand how you can use the skills, knowledge, and attitudes you develop in your psychology classes to become the person you want to become.

- You will learn about the skills that will enable you to perform well in academic settings (e.g., active learning and critical thinking) and how these skills will also benefit you in your post-baccalaureate future (e.g., on the job).

- You will learn about the knowledge that will help you make important future career decisions (e.g., what areas of specialization exist in psychology, what do psychologists in these areas do, and how much do they earn?)

- You will learn the types of attitudes and characteristics most valued by potential employers and graduate school admissions committees.

- You will learn strategies that will enable you to maximize the probability of obtaining the job to which you aspire or being accepted by the graduate school of your choice.

- You will become familiar with the ethical principles that psychologists use to guide their professional behaviors.

- You will learn about a variety of resources that can help you explore career possibilities in psychology, learn more about psychological organizations you can join, and discover sources from which you can learn more about psychology.

I wrote this book with you and your future in mind. Read it carefully, consider its advice wisely, and put its information to work as you begin to plan for your future.

Good luck!

CHAPTER 1

UNDERGRADUATE PSYCHOLOGY

Your undergraduate education is your chance to explore the myriad of opportunities that will be available to you. As a psychology major, you will be exposed to many different fields and courses, both within and outside of the psychology department. I encourage you to make the most of your education—four years will speed by!

WHAT IS PSYCHOLOGY?

Psychology is a science, an academic discipline, and a time-honored profession. This tripartite nature endows our discipline with a uniquely multifaceted nature. As **scientists**, we are concerned with the careful and systematic observation of behavior and the collection, analysis, and interpretation of empirical data. As **academics**, we deal in the abstract realm of theoretical interpretations and ethical controversies. As **professionals**, we are dedicated to improving the lives and preserving the dignity of our fellow men.

As you read this handbook, the panorama of psychology will open before you. You will learn about the opportunities and requirements of undergraduate studies, the challenges of careers and graduate education, and the rewards of a life dedicated to a discipline that is both rigorously scientific and genuinely humane. As you progress through your curriculum, you will discover those areas of specialization within psychology that will capture your interest and around which you can build your future.

Education is more than the mere accumulation of facts; it is the process of becoming a new person who is enlivened by the confidence gained from learning new ideas, mastering complex methods, and challenging difficult issues. Although educational values can be traced to the ancient Greeks, their strength is not their age, but their capacity for renewal. At the core of education is the development of ethical values, social responsibility, and a commitment to life-long learning.

Students who are drawn to psychology are those who wish to extend the boundaries of their knowledge, develop mature values, learn to distinguish between valuable and trivial information, and acquire the capacity and perspective necessary to understand and shape the world around them. They will gain from their studies a solid knowledge base of psychological terms, concepts, theories, methods, and issues. They will develop the ability to gather and synthesize information from a variety of sources—inside and outside the classroom.

Psychology requires advanced critical thinking skills in order to distill and evaluate this information and turn it into true knowledge. The study of psychology helps students to improve communication and interpersonal skills that will be invaluable in the future, wherever that may be.

Psychology is in a unique position because it serves as a type of bridge between the humanities and the sciences. Before you even begin your studies, it is important to recognize the very specific way in which you will be asked to think. You will be asked to practice **critical thinking,** and this type of thinking is really the foundation of all psychology courses. So this is where we will begin.

Critical thinking is the product of a combination of a set of interdependent cognitive **skills** and a firm commitment to a group of governing **attitudes** that enables individuals to use a variety of information and methods to make logical and objective decisions.

Critical thinking is at the very core of the study of psychology and its development is an essential part of an undergraduate education. The ability to think critically enables psychology students to extend the boundaries of their knowledge, develop mature values, learn to distinguish between valuable and trivial information, and acquire the capacity and perspective necessary to understand and shape the world around them. The following models of critical thinking skills and attitudes were developed to help psychology students become aware of the nature of this process and to value it, practice it, and exhibit it during their undergraduate experience.

THE SKILLS AND ATTITUDES OF A CRITICAL THINKER

Retention

Retention is the ability
- to remember specific information
- to acquire and retain specific psychological terms, definitions, facts, principles, and sequences
- to answer who, what, where, and when questions about psychology
- to remember facts, principles, and steps in sequences.
- sample question: *What is the definition of psychology?*

Comprehension

Comprehension is the ability
- to grasp the meaning of material
- to understand basic psychological principles, concepts, methods, and theories
- to answer how and why questions about psychology

- to explain, translate, or interpret to a new form or symbol system
- sample question: *Why is Wilhelm Wundt known as the founder of empirical psychology?*

Application

Application is the ability
- to use learned material to solve "real-life" problems
- to use psychological principles and methods to change behaviors and mental processes
- to perform psychological research and report the findings in a professional manner
- to use concepts, principles, and theories to finds solutions to problems
- sample question: *How can parents use extinction to decrease tantrums in their children?*

Analysis

Analysis is the ability
- to study a complicated whole by examining its parts and organizational structure
- to break down complex psychological principles, theories, and methods into their component parts
- to investigate the relationships that exist among the components of complex psychological phenomena
- to determine distinguishing characteristics and show the relationship among parts
- sample question: *Compare and contrast the humanistic and psychodynamic approaches to the explanation of personality.*

Synthesis

Synthesis is the ability
- to put parts together to form new and creative wholes
- to put together parts in order to form new wholes
- to produce unique and creative psychological ideas, solutions, hypotheses, and theories
- to combine previously learned material to produce new products (i.e., hypotheses)
- sample question: *Use the results of empirical research to answer the question: "Does watching violent television cause children to behave more aggressively?"*

Evaluation

Evaluation is the ability
- to judge the value of material for a given purpose
- to distinguish between fact and fiction, education and propaganda, relevant and irrelevant information, and rational and irrational thoughts and beliefs about psychology
- to identify and use valid criteria and methods during the processes of assessment, diagnosis, and research in psychology

- to make value judgments, rate ideas, and accept or reject materials based on valid criteria
- sample question: *Use the criteria discussed in class to assess the validity of Freud's theory.*

Attitudes

The following is a partial list of the attitudes that foster successful critical thinking.
- Critical thinking is hard work requiring courage to begin and persistence to complete.
- Careful and systematic planning is a prerequisite for any complex intellectual undertaking.
- Errors provide valuable feedback, and knowledge of their causes is a foundation for future success.
- Terms and issues must be clearly defined before they can be discussed meaningfully and productively.
- For every major issue, there are many different points of view, and all sides of an issue must be investigated thoroughly before a conclusion is reached. To be perceived as intellectually responsible, individuals must make every effort to understand the perspectives of those with whom they disagree.
- An attitude of healthy skepticism is a valuable tool, especially when confronted with slanted, selective, prejudiced, or self-justifying information.
- The assumptions of a theory, tradition, or belief must be analyzed carefully and understood completely before it can be either accepted or rejected.
- It is perfectly acceptable, and often highly desirable, for individuals to change their beliefs, values, or behaviors if presented with sufficient empirical evidence or logical justification to do so.
- Those with whom we agree are not always right and those with whom we disagree are not always wrong. When disagreeing, it is best to do so in an agreeable manner—disagreements should produce constructive discussions, not arguments.
- There are no simplistic, dogmatic explanations of complex phenomena. It is often necessary to look beyond obvious, common sense, or traditional answers to discover valid causal relationships.
- Many theories can be used to explain behavior. The theory an individual chooses to embrace is dependent upon that individual's unique set of academic, cultural, spiritual, methodological, professional, and personal values.
- Many methods can be used to study behavior (e.g., experiments, correlational studies, naturalistic observations, or case studies). The appropriateness of a particular method is determined by a careful determination of its purpose and the individuals, situations, and ethical principles involved.
- Learning is a life-long process that can occur in the absence of any formal educational process—critical thinkers learn from their teachers, but they can also learn by themselves long after their formal education has ceased.

POTENTIAL COURSES

With the model of critical thinking in mind, let's take this time to get an overview of the kinds of courses that you will encounter in you undergraduate education, both in psychology and in other disciplines. There are certain psychology courses that are required for majors at almost any school, and there are some that will be offered on an elective basis. Spend plenty of time choosing your courses—talk to advisors and to friends who may have taken the class before. Remember that it is important to try to get a well-rounded education, so keep an open mind and don't be afraid to try something that is new to you! The lists that follow on the next few pages are samples—check your course bulletin to see what is offered at your school.

Sample Listing of Psychology Courses

Abnormal Psychology
Behavioral Neuroscience
Biology of Behavior
Clinical Psychology
Cognitive Psychology
Counseling Psychology
Directed Research
Experimental Psychology
General Psychology
History of Psychology
Human Growth and Development
Human Information Processing

Independent Study
Internship in Psychology
Psychology of Gender
Psychology of Learning
Psychology of Motivation
Sensation and Perception
Social Psychology
Sports Psychology
Statistical Methods
Stress Management
Tests and Measurement
Theories of Personality

Standard Offerings in Psychology Departments

You will probably not, in your four years as an undergraduate, be able to take all of the above psychology courses. The following is a standard program of psychology courses for a Bachelor of Arts in psychology. Keep in mind, once again, that this is only a sample, and that the specifics will vary from school to school.

Required Classes (all six must be successfully completed)
PSY 101 - General Psychology
PSY 205 - Statistical Methods
PSY 250 - Experimental Methods in Psychology
PSY 300 - Psychological Tests and Measurement
PSY 375 - History of Psychology
PSY 490 - Senior Seminar in Psychology

Psychology as a Social Science (at least two must be completed)
PSY 220 - Human Growth and Developmental
PSY 230 - Abnormal Psychology
PSY 325 - Social Psychology
PSY 335 - Theories of Personality

Psychology as a Natural Science (at least two must be completed)
PSY 305 - Psychology of Learning
PSY 315 - Psychology of Motivation
PSY 345 - Human Information Processing
PSY 350 - Behavioral Neuroscience

Senior Independent Work, Research, etc.

Electives

A psychology major cannot survive on psychology courses alone. It is also important during the college years to clarify and develop personal values, and to gain insight into the factors that determine individual and social behavior. One hopes that an undergraduate student will begin to explore relationships that govern nature and the physical world. It is important to be able to identify and deal with contemporary problems and the issues that affect the world around you. In order to understand the present, it is necessary to appreciate the past—the heritage of western and non-western cultures, and their various contributions and interdependence. The following list indicates the areas that you should consider in order to stay on the road to a well-rounded education. I have also included a more specific list of courses that would fall into each of the categories, to give you an idea of the types of electives that you can expect to encounter in your undergraduate education. Each in their own way, they will help you to improve your skills of reasoning, critical thinking, contemplation, and communication.

English composition
Fundamentals of speech
One class in theology
One class in philosophy
One class in history
One class in sociology
A general humanities class
One lab class in a natural science
    (biology, chemistry, physics)

One class in art history or appreciation
One class in music history or appreciation
At least two years of a foreign language
One logic, math, or computer science class
One economics or political science class
Two classes on non-western culture
One class in advanced literature
One class (not necessarily a lab) from the
    same natural science choices

Some Sample Electives

Art
    Art Appreciation
    Introduction to Art Therapy

Biology
    Anatomy and Physiology
    Genetics
    Ecology
    Evolution

Business
    Principles of Marketing
    Principles of Advertising
    Management
    Organizational Behavior
    Personnel Management

Chemistry
    Elements of General and Biological Chemistry
    Inorganic Chemistry
    Organic Chemistry

College-Wide Electives
    Excelling in College
    Career Exploration

Computer Science
    Introduction to Computer Systems
    Programming I
    Desk Top Publishing
    Integrated Software and Communications
    Computer Graphics and Video
    Database Management
    Systems Analysis

Dietetics
    Human Nutrition
    Consumer Behavior

Economics
    Introductory Economics

Education
   Introduction to Exceptional Children
   Educational Psychology
   Early Childhood Guidance
   The Mildly Handicapped: Learning Problems

English
   Creative Writing
   Major American Authors
   The English Language
   English Literature II
   Twentieth Century Novel
   Twentieth Century Poetry and Drama
   Business and Technical Writing

Health and Physical Education
   Weight Training (or any other PE activity course)
   First Aid

History
   United States History
   Modern European History
   Introduction to the Non-Western World

Journalism
   Introduction to Mass Media
   News Writing

Mathematics
   Intermediate Algebra
   College Algebra
   Probability and Statistics

Music
   Appreciation of Music

Philosophy
   Logic
   General Ethics
   Philosophy of Man and Knowledge
   Philosophy of Being (Metaphysics)

Political Science
   American Politics
   International Relations

Sociology
   Volunteer Service
   Social Problems
   Child, Family, and Society
   Minority Groups
   The Family
   Criminology
   Cultural Anthropology
   Social Gerontology

Speech
   Persuasion and Debate
   Business and Professional Communications

Theater
   Introduction to the Theater
   Beginning Acting

Theology
   Moral Issues
   Psychology of Religion

YOUR SCHEDULE

Your studies will consist of a combination of psychology courses and electives. The following is a sample four-year schedule for a psychology major.

FRESHMAN YEAR

Fall Semester

General Psychology
Excelling in College
English Composition
Foreign Language/Elective
Mathematics
Economics or Political Science

Spring Semester

Human Growth/Development
Anatomy and Physiology
Fundamentals of Speech
Foreign Language/Elective
Sociology

SOPHOMORE YEAR

Fall Semester

Statistical Methods
Humanities I
Introduction to Theology
Foreign Language/Elective
History

Spring Semester

Experimental Psychology
Humanities II
Cognitive Psychology
Foreign Language/Elective
Nonwest Studies

JUNIOR YEAR

Fall Semester

Theories of Personality
Behavioral Neuroscience
Chemistry, Biology, or Physics
Two Electives

Spring Semester

Introduction to Philosophy
Psychological Measurement
History of Psychology
Two Electives

SENIOR YEAR

Fall Semester

Senior Seminar in Psychology
Four Electives

Spring Semester

Internship in Psychology
Four Electives

SKILLS FOR SUCCESS IN PSYCHOLOGY

In this section, I will discuss some of the specific skills that will help you in your courses, both psychology and non-psychology. You should remember, of course, that **critical thinking** is the foundation for all of the skills involved in your educational experience.

Skill #1: Active Learning

Adopt the attitude that your college teachers are responsible for no more than presenting ideas and information to you—and that it is your responsibility to learn. Students are often conditioned by magazines, television, and movies to be **passive** learners, and therefore they expect to be entertained by their textbooks and instructors. Education is serious business, and you cannot afford to approach it in the same way that you would approach the recreational media.

Enter each class the attitude that you are going to become an **active** learner, and that you are going to get the most out of every class. You have paid your money, so get what you paid for. You are the consumer! You can make even the most boring class interesting by assuming that every teacher has useful information for you. Be determined to learn everything that you can from each of your teachers and textbooks. Remember—the best investment that you will ever make is in yourself (Walter and Siebert, 1993).

It goes without saying that attending class is the first step in a commitment to active learning. The following is a list of the passive options that are to be avoided and the active steps to take instead that will help you get the most out of your education.

Passive: Just sit in lectures because you have to be there.
Active: Come to lectures prepared, pay attention, take notes, and ask questions.

Passive: Buy used books that already have the important points underlined.
Active: Buy new books and do the underlining yourself.

Passive: Borrow and use lectures notes from someone who have already taken the class.
Active: Take you own lecture notes.

Passive: Read assignments just to get them over with.
Active: Skim assignments first, make up a list of questions that you would like to answer, and then read the assignments to answer the questions.

Passive: Pay attention only to the grades you earned on tests when they are returned.
Active : Study returned tests carefully so that you don't make the same mistakes again.

ACTIVE VS. PASSIVE LEARNING STYLE TEST
(from Walter and Siebert, 1993)

In each pair of statements below, place a check mark on the line to the left of the statement that you believe is true. Try to be as honest as possible in all of your choices.

1. ____Promotions are earned with hard work and persistence.　　　　____Promotions come from knowing the right people.

2. ____I would get better grades if my teachers were better.　　　　____How hard I study determines the grades I get.

3. ____The increasing divorce rate indicates that fewer people are trying to make their marriages last.　　　　____Fate determines how long a marriage will last. All you can do is hope that your partner will stay with you for life.

4. ____It is useless to try to change the attitudes and behaviors of others.　　　　____I can usually change others to see and do things my way.

5. ____In our society, a person's income is determined primarily by his or her level of ability and motivation　　　　____Finding a well-paying job is simply a matter of being luckier than other people.

6. ____Many people are hard to get along with and there is no use trying to be friendly to them.　　　　____Getting along with people is a skill that can be learned over time with a little patience.

7. ____My grades are a result of my own effort, not luck.　　　　____Whether I study or not has little effect on my grades.

8. ____It is wishful thinking to believe that one person can change what happens in society today.　　　　____People like me can change the course of events by standing up and making themselves heard.

9. ____The good and bad things that happen to me are determined primarily by what I do.　　　　____When I see an unfortunate person, I sometimes think, "There, but for the grace of God, go I."

10. ____I would be so much happier if life weren't so stressful.　　　　____Peace of mind comes from learning to adapt to the stresses of life.

To score your test, add the check marks in the left column for the odd-numbered items (1, 3, 5, etc.) and in the right column for the even-numbered items. The higher your score, the more likely you are to be an active learner. If your score is particularly low, you may want to reconsider your beliefs about who is responsible for your ability to learn and perform well in your classes and change your attitudes and behaviors accordingly. Remember, it's your education and *only you* can make it what you want it to be.

Passive: Don't work any harder than you have to in any class.
Active :   Volunteer to help someone in your class who is having a tough time.

There are some actions, of course, that are negative rather than positive and that detract severely from the learning process. The following list points out a few such activities. This may seem like stating the obvious, but you will be surprised by the number of students who continue to take part in behaviors that they know are detrimental.

Behaviors Interpreted by Teachers as Rude or Disrespectful
- talking during lectures
- being late
- chewing gum, eating, or drinking noisily
- creating disturbances
- wearing hats
- obvious yawning
- slouching in seats
- putting feet on desks or tables
- sleeping
- cutting class
- acting bored or apathetic
- not paying attention
- being unprepared
- packing-up books and materials before class is over
- asking already-answered questions
- sitting in the back when there are empty seats in the front
- asking "Did we do anything important?" after missing class
- asking "Will it be on the test?"
- being more interested in grades than in learning
- not asking questions
- being insincere (i.e., "brown-nosing")
- complaining about work load
- blaming teachers for poor grades
- giving unbelievable excuses
- doing work for other classes in class
- acting like a know-it-all
- not asking for help or asking for help when it is too late

Skill #2: Reading a Text

It is important to feel familiar and comfortable with your textbook before you begin your semester's work. Take the time to read the introduction, to discover the author's approach, style, and academic background. Familiarize yourself with the organizational structure and the pedagogical aids, such as the table of contents, the chapter outlines, the use of boldfaced terms, the chapter and section summaries, appendixes, and glossary. Then, when you receive your first assignment, you will be prepared to complete it in the most effective and efficient way possible.

As you read an assignment, keep the following questions in mind. Do I really understand this? If the answer is no, then go back and figure out where you got lost and review the material from that point. The SQ4R method that is outlined below has these checks built into it, but you have to self-check yourself constantly to make sure that you are getting the most out of your textbook. Remember also that the SQ4R method is intended to act only as a *general* guideline. You may use some or all aspects of the method—try out different combinations and see what works for you. Reading and learning are ultimately individual endeavors, and each person takes in information in different ways. The more familiar you are with your mental processes, the more successfully you can use them to your academic advantage.

The SQ4R Method

1. **Survey** — should take only 5-10 minutes for a 50-page chapter and save 25 percent of study time
   a. chapter title
   b. chapter outline
   c. introduction or first paragraph
   d. section headings
   e. illustrations and their captions
   f. section summaries
   g. questions at the end of the chapter

2. **Question**
   a. Write questions you would like to answer from the assignment on 3x5 cards—Reading becomes more purposeful if you have questions to answer.
   b. Do not overload yourself with questions and do not make your questions to elaborate.
   c. Be flexible; add, omit, or change your questions if necessary.

3. **Read**
   a. Read until you come to the answer of a question.
   b. Study the answer and try to understand it in your own words.

4. **Recite**
   a. Close the book.
   b. Repeat the answer back to yourself in your own words.
   c. Open the book, and compare your answer to the book's answer.
   d. If it is not acceptable, go back to the last step and repeat it.
   e. If it is acceptable, move on.

5. **Write**
    a. Write the answer to the question (and page number) on the reverse side of the card.
    b. Repeat steps 3–5 until you have written all the answers to your questions.

6. **Review**
    a. Use the cards as flash cards.
    b. Review immediately after finishing the assignment.
    c. Review at least three more times, once immediately before the test.

Textbooks are expensive, and smart students get their money's worth from them. Always approach an assignment with specific goals in mind—know what you want to get out of the assignment and know how to get it. Be able to differentiate between the important ideas and the supplementary details— highlight the main ideas so that your review process can be efficient and productive. (Use your pen or your highlighter wisely—too many lines can be distracting). Remember that people learn best when they experience new material in a number of ways—reading, reciting, and writing the answers to your questions will help you learn the information in an assignment more effectively than just reading it. For instance, writing answers to questions you have constructed is an excellent method to prepare for a test.

After you feel that you have learned the material, try to apply it to your own life experiences. Meaningful and personally relevant information is learned more quickly and retained longer than material perceived to be meaningless or irrelevant. And the final words of advice are **practice, practice, practice**. When you think you know your material, go back and review it again a few hours or even a few days later. Learning takes times, and no amount of strategizing and planning can replace hard work.

Skill #3: Writing an APA Style Paper

Writing papers will be a major part of your coursework, so it is a good idea to establish a formula that you can always follow. By using the following method, the structure of the paper will be taken care of, leaving you plenty of time to concentrate on the content!

General Guidelines*
- Papers should be word-processed with one-inch margins left-right and top-bottom.
- A cover sheet should include the title, author, course, instructor, and date.
- Use centered headings to separate major sections of a paper and left-justified and underlined headings to separate sub-sections within major sections.
- Use the spell- and grammar-checkers in your word processor to help you proofread.
- Have a friend read your paper and point out parts that are unclear.
- Secure the paper with a staple. Do not use report covers.
- Keep a copy of your paper. Do not submit a paper unless you have a copy.

How to Cite References in the Body of A Paper
- The last name of the author(s) and the year of publication of a reference are inserted in the body of a paper at appropriate points to give credit for ideas other than your own. This may be done in the following ways:

  a. If an author's name appears in a sentence, cite the year in parentheses:
     1) Daugherty (1992) concluded . . .
     2) Wittekind, Hingtgen, Gheen, and Appleby (1991) found . . . (first citation)
     3) Wittekind, et al. (1991) also found . . . (subsequent citations)
  b. Otherwise, both the name and the year appear in parentheses:
     1) ...has been found (Camp & Appleby, 1989).
     2) In a recent study of retention (Plascak-Craig, 1991), it was found that...
  c. If different authors are cited at the same point, use the following format:
     1) Recent studies (Adams, 1987; Camp, 1986; Wittekind, 1989) show . . .

- If a paper includes a direct quote from a reference, enclose the quote in quotation marks and cite the source including the author, year, and page number:

  a. "Dreams reveal facets of an individual's personality" (Wittekind, 1989, p. 43).
  b. Wittekind (1989) stated that, "Dreams reveal facets of an individual's personality" (p. 43).

How To Cite References in the Reference Section of a Paper
- **Books**
  Adams, R. W. (1977). Leaving academia. Phoenix, AZ: Liberation Press.
- **Journal Articles**
  Carlson, C. W. (1984). Advertising Power. Consumer Psychology, 17, 62-69.
- **Magazine Articles**
  Trexler, L. D. (1994, August). Injured brains. Psychology Today, pp. 56-59.

- **Articles or Chapters in an Edited Book**
  Hingtgen, J. N. (1986). Opera-induced deafness. In B. Sills & L. Pavarotti (Eds.), <u>Progress in musical psychology</u> (pp. 239-252). New York: Academic Press.

Note: An Ampersand (&) is used to connect multiple authors in the reference section and within parentheses in the body of a paper.

*These guidelines are a modified version of those written by Dr. Michael Stevenson of Ball State University.

Skill # 4: Efficient Note-Taking

Note-taking is a central part of the active learning process—the act of writing down the information that the professor is giving you helps you to retain the material. When you take notes, you become a participant in the class rather than a passive listener. You will be better able to keep your attention focused and mind engaged. Note-taking requires that you mentally organize the lecture's content, that you pick out the main points and the important terms and concepts. You will be able to enhance your listening skills and learn how to process information quickly. Finally, the notes that you take during a lecture will be absolutely essential when test time comes around and you need to review.

Learn how your professors communicate to you that something is important. The following are some methods professor use to communicate important points. Watch out for these or other signals!
- Repetition
- Becoming still (stop pacing)
- Making eye contact
- Giving several examples
- Writing on the board
- Make dramatic gestures.
- Changing their tone of voice.
- Saying "in summary" or "in conclusion."
- Giving you time to write in your notes.
- Following a point with a period of dramatic silence.
- Including a point in their introduction to a lecture.

Try hard to understand the organizational structure of lectures.
- Pay close attention during introductions and summaries.
- Use the outline method of note-taking whenever possible.

Develop a "speed hand."
- Use abbreviations.
- Keep a list of your abbreviations and their meanings.

Date your notes.
- This helps to keep them in order if you remove pages from your notebook.
- Dating pages makes it easier for professors to answer your questions if you can tell them the date of the lecture.

Six principles of efficient note-taking:
1. Be flexible; adapt your note-taking style to different lecturing styles.
2. Once you select a successful style, stay with it.
3. Schedule a time as soon after class as possible to review your notes.
4. Take no more notes than are necessary for complete understanding.
5. Use your "speed hand" whenever possible.
6. Your notes should be immediately clear when you re-read them; if they are not, ask a reliable fellow student, the teaching assistant, or your professor for clarification as soon as possible.

In conclusion, remember the importance of active learning. Do not attend class just so the professor won't count you absent. Go to class prepared to learn actively the material that will be given in lecture. Pay close attention to the professor, notice what he says and what he does, and do your best to understand the overall organization of the lecture. Do your best to pick up the subtle, and sometimes the not-so-subtle, cues that your professors give during their lectures that indicate that they are discussing an important point. Try to experience new information in a variety of ways—first listen to your professor, then think about what she's saying, then see the information as you write it down. It is important to re-read your notes as soon as possible after class and to review them several times before the test. Remember that you and your professor are in a learning partnership, but also know that it is **you** who must take ultimate responsibility for your education.

Skill #5: Taking the Test

There are basically two types of test that you will encounter as an undergraduate psychology student. One type is the **objective test,** so called because the answer to a question is either right or wrong, regardless of who is grading the test. Objective tests include matching, true/false, multiple choice, and fill-in-the-blank. The material that is tested is purely factual and can often be learned by memorization. Skills that are important for success on an objective test are recognition and decision making.

The other type of test is the **subjective test,** and the answers to this kind of test are, as you can imagine, subject to personal interpretation. Certain information must be present, of course, but the quality of the answer is judged by the grader. Scores therefore vary depending on the characteristics of the grader. Subjective test questions are answered either in essay form or in a short answer (usually one or two paragraphs). The material that is tested is conceptual and theoretical and requires an advanced understanding of the topic. Skills that are important for success on a subjective test include comprehension, application, analysis, synthesis, and evaluation.

Of course, many psychology tests are actually a combination of objective and subjective questions. This is often the most effective type of test because it evaluates both factual retention and theoretical understanding. Both types of learning are crucial to achieve a full appreciation of psychology.

Preparation Strategies for Objective Tests
1. Increase retention of new material
    a. Use SQ4R cards as flash cards.
    b. Quiz classmates on key terms and concepts.
    c. Use mnemonics (i.e., memory strategies).

2. Increase understanding of new material
    a. Make up concrete examples of abstract ideas.
    b. Apply new material to your everyday life.

3. Anticipate questions and avoid mistakes
    a. Review and learn from previous tests in the class.
    b. Try to identify reasons why you missed previous questions.

Test Taking Strategies for Objective Tests
1. Read directions carefully and ask for clarification if necessary.
2. Read all questions thoroughly before you answer any of them.
3. Answer the easiest questions first and leave the hardest for last.
4. Read all the answers to each question before you select one.
5. Use the process of elimination to increase your success on hard questions.
6. Don't be fooled by absolutes (questions that make claims about "everyone" or "never").
7. Use remaining time to check answers.
8. Answer changing is okay, but know your answer-changing style.
9. If your professor allows you to write on the test paper, cross out wrong answers and underline critical words in the questions to help you focus on the right answer.

Preparation Strategies for Subjective Tests
1. Attempt to anticipate questions (2nd step of SQ4R).
2. Practice writing answers to anticipated questions (4th step of SQ4R).
3. Use mnemonics to help you remember main parts of answers.
4. Review previous tests in the class to help you identify weaknesses in your pattern of answering subjective test questions.

Test-Taking Strategies for Subjective Tests
1. Read directions carefully and ask for clarification if necessary.
2. Determine how much time to spend on each question.
3. Begin with the easiest question.
4. Underline important parts of the question, and be sure to answer all the parts.
5. Prepare a brief outline of your answer.
6. Write your answer and check off outline points as you write.
7. Go to next easiest question and follow steps three to five and continue with the remaining questions.
8. Spend the final 10 minutes reviewing your answers to detect and correct any errors in facts, grammar, or spelling.

General Strategies for Both Types of Tests (Preparation + Control = Success)
1. Preparation before tests
    a. Attend classes without fail.
    b. Listen actively during lectures and take careful notes.
    c. Use the SQ4R method to read assignments.
    d. Divide study time into sections; do not cram.
    e. Study questions you missed on old tests so you can avoid missing them on future tests.
    f. Review both alone and with others in the class, but remember that study sessions that are primarily social will not help your test scores.

2. Control during tests
    a. Read all questions first.
    b. Ask your professor for clarification of questions.
    c. Answer the easiest questions first.
    d. Use the process of elimination (objective tests).
    e. Outline answers (subjective tests).
    f. Review and check answers.

3. Success before, during, and after tests
    a. You will acquire, understand, and retain new and valuable knowledge.
    b. You will achieve higher academic performance in the form of better grades.
    c. You will increase your sense of self-esteem.

Taking a test can be the most stressful but also the most rewarding part of the active learning process. The test is your chance to show your professor just how hard you have been working and how well you have absorbed the course material. Take studying for the test seriously, but try to avoid excessive anxiety. One way to maintain this balance is to spread your studying over several short sessions rather than one long sitting. In other words, **avoid cramming**. You should feel familiar with the material when you begin the test, and you cannot feel comfortable with information that you stuffed into your head all at once. It is important also to feel comfortable with the test itself and with the test-taking environment. Don't go into the first test in any class without having an idea of what it will be like. Try to find out about your professor's testing methods by asking students who have done well in the class before. Old tests are often available for examination—this is a great way to familiarize yourself with the test's structure and feel. As the semester goes on, you will find that much can be learned from studying **your** old tests. Many psychology concepts build on ideas that came before, and by looking at your old tests, you can be certain that you understand the past material before you move onto the new material. Pay very close attention to the questions that you missed, and make sure that you have the correct answer. Also take note of the types of questions that gave you a hard time and spend extra time preparing for that type of question for the next test.

Do not expect learning to be a quick and easy process. It will take time and sometimes it will be difficult. Expect to spend a minimum of one and a half hours studying and writing papers outside of class for each hour of class that you attend. In other words, think about college as a full-time job in which you must put in at least forty hours of concentrated academic work per week (16 hours in class and another 24 hours of studying outside class). That still leaves you with 128 hours to eat, sleep, socialize, play, and relax each week! So even though learning can be frustrating sometimes, if you work hard you can make it an important part of a full and enriching life.

LOOKING AHEAD

Although education has many immediate benefits, there is always the important question: What is my education going to do for me once I get out of school? We will go into the specifics of job hunting and graduate school applications later on in this handbook. At this time, we will simply discuss the ways in which your future plans should shape your approach to undergraduate education.

The two most common options available to college graduates are finding a job or going to graduate school. Therefore, a question they often ask their academic advisers is: "How do I get into graduate school?" or "How do I get a job?" These questions should be addressed early in an undergraduate's college career because the answers are often very unpleasant if the student has not engaged in appropriate career-planning activities during the freshman and sophomore years and carried through on these plans as a junior and senior.

The **first** step in this process involves the student's decision to pursue either a career that requires a graduate degree or else a job in a field for which graduate education is unnecessary. The **second** step is to determine the set of factors that will increase the probability of success in that career plan. The **third** step is to maximize these factors. To assist academic advisers in their attempt to help students answer these questions and maximize their chances of post-graduate success, Milton, Pollio, & Eison (1986) performed a survey of "362 representatives of business and industry who were actively involved in interviewing and hiring college graduates" and 500 college faculty from the areas of natural science, social science, the humanities, and pre-professional programs. The task of the members of these samples was to rate the importance of each of the factors in the following 15 item lists on a 1 to 7 scale depending upon "the value or degree of importance they placed on each of the 15 possible pieces of information when reviewing the materials submitted by recent college graduates for either employment in their firm or for admission to graduate school." The two following lists are arranged in descending order of these ratings.

Business Representatives	College Faculty
1. Personality of student	1. Grades in major courses
2. Grades in major courses	2. Number of difficult courses
3. Nature of non-college jobs	3. Samples of student writing
4. Overall grade point average	4. Letters of recommendation
5. Breadth of courses taken	5. Publications, honors, awards
6. School/Recommender reputation	6. Breadth of courses taken
7. Breadth of life experiences	7. School/Recommender reputation
8. Extracurricular activities	8. Standardized test scores
9. Publications, awards, honors	9. Overall grade point average
10. Number of difficult courses	10. Breadth of life experiences
11. Samples of student writing	11. Personality of student
12. Affirmative action needs	12. Contributions to the school
13. Contributions to the school	13. Extracurricular activities
14. Letters of recommendation	14. Nature of non-college jobs
15. Standardized test scores	15. Affirmative action needs

It appears from these lists that employers and graduate schools put emphasis on very different factors when they weigh the qualifications of newly-graduated college students. A quick check of the top five factors indicates that employers appear to be most impressed with job applicants who possess a good personality, earn high grades in both their majors and a wide variety of other courses, and have relevant employment experience outside the college environment. Graduate schools are most impressed with undergraduates who earn high grades in their majors, take difficult courses, are good writers, earn high recommendations, and have publications, honors, or awards to their credit. Undergraduates should study these lists very carefully during the early stages of their college careers when they are engaged in initial career-planning activities. Their willingness and ability to attain these factors successfully will have a profound effect upon their chances of post-graduate success.

Regardless of whether you decide to apply to graduate school or to look for a job right after receiving your bachelor's degree, it is important to approach your education with an overall schedule or plan that encompasses all four years. The following sample time-line gives you an idea of the various steps that you should take each of the four years in order to prepare for life after college.

The idea of planning for your future when you are still trying to figure out about the present of college life can be intimidating, to say the least. No one, however, expects you to do all of this on your own. No matter what kind of school you are attending, whether it is the largest state university or the smallest liberal arts college, there is always some sort of support system in place—it is just a question of finding it. It can even be said that this handbook is a type of mentoring, as it is a means of passing down knowledge that extends beyond the information that you can find in a textbook. Whatever the shape your support system takes, informal or formal, the same basic idea will be behind it—the idea of the mentor.

Mentoring (the verb form of mentor) has its etymological roots in *The Odyssey*, Homer's epic poem. The poem's hero (Odysseus) was a great warrior who left his son (Telemachus) in the care of a trusted friend (Mentor) while he was fighting the Trojan War. Mentor fulfilled his role admirably as he served Telemachus as both loyal guardian and wise adviser. As the story unfolded, Mentor led Telemachus on the heroic journey to find his lost father during which Telemachus matured and developed his own identity.

Shandley (1989) has drawn the following conclusions from the historical derivation of the term "mentoring" and uses the term "protégé" to describe the person who is the recipient in the mentoring process. First, it is the intentional process of interaction between at least two individuals, requiring specific action on both parts. Second, mentoring is a nurturing process that fosters the growth and development of the protégé toward full maturity. Third, mentoring is an insightful process in which the wisdom of the mentor is acquired and applied by the protégé. Fourth, mentoring is a supportive, often protective process. The mentor can serve as an important guide or reality-checker in introducing the protégé to the environment for which he or she is preparing. Finally, it is also reasonable to conclude that an essential component of serving as a mentor is role modeling. Although it is wrong to suggest that a protégé should become a clone of his or her mentor, mentors need to make themselves available as models, exposing both what they have done well, as well as what could have been done better (p. 60). "Mentoring is a way of individualizing a student's education by allowing or encouraging the student to connect with a college staff member who is experienced in a particular field or set of skills. The mentor must care enough about the student to take time to teach, to show, to challenge, and to support" (Lester & Johnson, 1981, p. 50).

I hope that this handbook does indeed serve as one of your mentors as you make your way through your undergraduate education. In the next two chapters, we will turn our attention to preparation for graduate school and for the job search.

CHAPTER 2

GRADUATE SCHOOL

Many of you are entering the psychology department because you want to become psychologists or psychiatrists. A career in one of these fields requires education above and beyond a bachelor's degree. Graduate school is not for everyone, but for those who are the right match, it can be a stimulating and enriching experience.

AN OVERVIEW

Each psychology major approaches graduate school with different expectations and varying ultimate goals. They all have in some things in common, however—a dedication to the discipline of psychology and a desire to deepen their understanding. In addition, most people who enter graduate school do so with a specific career path in mind, even though that path may be altered over the course of their years in school. In the following pages, I will try to give you an idea of the variety of careers available to you as well as some of the steps that you will have to take to achieve your career goals.

To give you the broadest possible look at psychology-oriented careers, I have drawn on several different sources and given you their impressions in their own words. Keep in mind, of course, that their experiences and ideas are not universal, and that you will have to do your own research to find out about specific careers and schools that interest you. Still, some general rules apply, and the following pages should help to introduce you to them.

The Occupational Outlook Handbook is a wonderful source of information for undergraduates that provides them with valuable information about their occupational choices. The information in this section is taken verbatim from the psychology section the 1994-95 edition of this publication.

What Do Psychologists Do?

Nature of the Work. Psychologists study human behavior and mental processes to describe, understand, predict, and change people's behavior. They may study the way a person thinks, feels, or behaves. Research psychologists investigate the physical, cognitive, emotional, or social aspects of human behavior. Psychologists in applied fields counsel and conduct training programs; do market research; apply psychological treatments to a variety of medical and surgical conditions; or provide mental health services in hospitals, clinics, or private settings.

Like other social scientists, psychologists formulate hypotheses and collect data to test their validity. Research methods depend on the topic under study. Psychologists may gather information through controlled laboratory experiments; personality, performance, aptitude, and intelligence tests; observation, interviews, and questionnaires; clinical studies; or surveys. Computers are widely used to record and analyze this information.

Since psychology deals with human behavior, psychologists apply their knowledge and techniques to a wide range of endeavors including human services, management, education, law, and sports. In addition to the variety of work settings, psychologists specialize in many different areas. *Clinical psychologists*, who constitute the largest specialty, generally work in independent or group practice or in hospitals or clinics. They may help the mentally or emotionally disturbed adjust to life, and are increasingly helping all kinds of medical and surgical patients deal with their illnesses or injuries. They may work in physical medicine and rehabilitation settings, treating patients with spinal cord injuries, chronic pain or illness, stroke and arthritis and neurologic conditions, such as multiple sclerosis. Others help people deal with life stresses such as divorce or aging. Clinical psychologists interview patients; give diagnostic tests; provide individual, family, and group psychotherapy; and design and implement behavior modification programs. They may collaborate with physicians and other specialists in developing treatment programs, and help patients understand and comply with the prescribed treatment. Some clinical psychologists work in universities, where they train graduate students in the delivery of mental health and behavioral medicine services. Others administer community mental health programs. *Counseling psychologists* use several techniques, including interviewing and testing, to advise people on how to deal with problems of everyday living-personal, social, educational, or vocational.

Developmental psychologists study the patterns and causes of behavioral change as people progress through life from infancy to adulthood. Some concern themselves with behavior during infancy, childhood, and adolescence, while others study changes that take place during maturity and old age. The study of developmental disabilities and how they affect a person and others is a new area within developmental psychology. *Educational psychologists* evaluate student and teacher needs, and design and develop programs to enhance the educational setting. *Experimental psychologists* study behavior processes, and work with human beings and animals such as rats, monkeys, and pigeons. Prominent areas of experimental research include motivation, thinking, attention, learning and retention, sensory and perceptual processes, effects of substance use and abuse, and genetic and neurological factors in behavior.

Industrial and organizational psychologists apply psychological techniques to personnel administration, management, and marketing problems. They are involved in policy planning, applicant screening, training and development, psychological test research, counseling, and organizational development and analysis. For example, an industrial psychologist may work with management to develop better training programs and to reorganize the work setting to improve worker productivity or quality of worklife. *School psychologists* examine people's interactions with others and with the social environment. Prominent areas of study include group behavior, leadership, attitudes and interpersonal perception.

Some relatively new specialties include cognitive psychology, health psychology, neuropsychology, and geropsychology. *Cognitive psychologists* deal with the brain's role in memory, thinking, and perceptions; some are involved with research related to computer programming and artificial intelligence. *Health psychologists* promote good health through health maintenance counseling programs that are designed, for example, to help people stop smoking or lose weight. *Neuropsychologists* study the relation between the brain and behavior. They often work in stroke and head injury programs. *Geropsychologists* deal with the special problems faced by the elderly. The emergence and growth of these specialties reflects the increasing participation of psychologists in providing direct services to special patient populations.

Other areas of specialization include psychometrics, psychology and the arts, history of psychology, psychopharmacology, and community, comparative, consumer, engineering, environmental, family, forensic, population, military, and rehabilitation psychology.

Working Conditions. A psychologist's specialty and place of employment determine working conditions. For example, clinical, school, and counseling psychologists in private practice have pleasant, comfortable offices and set their own hours. However, they often have evening hours to accommodate their clients. Some employed in hospitals, nursing homes, and other health facilities often work evenings and weekends, while others in schools and clinics work regular hours. Psychologists employed by academic institutions divide their time among teaching, research, and administrative responsibilities. Some maintain part-time consulting practices as well. In contrast to the many psychologist who have flexible work schedules, most in government and private industry have more structured schedules. They often work alone, reading and writing research reports. Many experience deadlines, tight schedules, and overtime work. Their routine may be interrupted frequently. Travel may be required to attend conferences or conduct research.

Employment. Psychologists held about 144,000 jobs in 1992. Educational institutions employed nearly 4 out of 10 salaried psychologists in positions involving counseling, testing, special education, research, and administration; hospitals, mental health clinics, rehabilitation centers, nursing homes, and other health facilities employed 3 out of 10; and government agencies at the federal, state, and local levels employed one-sixth. The Department of Veterans Affairs, the Department of Defense, and the Public health Service employ the overwhelming majority of psychologists working for federal agencies. Governments employ psychologists in hospitals, clinics, correctional facilities, and other settings. Psychologists also work in social service organizations, research organizations, management consulting firms, marketing research firms, and other businesses.

After several years of experience, some psychologists, usually those with doctoral degrees, enter private practice or set up their own research or consulting firms. A growing proportion of psychologists are self-employed.

Besides the jobs described above, many persons held positions as psychology faculty at colleges and universities, and as high school psychology teachers.

Training, Other Qualifications, and Advancement. A **doctoral degree** generally is required for employment as a psychologist. Psychologists with a Ph.D. qualify for a wide range of teaching, research, clinical, and counseling positions in universities, elementary and secondary schools, private industry, and government. Psychologists with a Psy.D. (Doctor of Psychology) qualify mainly for clinical positions.

Persons with a **master's degree** in psychology can administer tests as psychological assistants. Under the supervision of doctoral level psychologists, they can conduct research in laboratories, conduct psychological evaluations, counsel patients, or perform administrative duties. They may teach in high schools or 2-year colleges or work as school psychologists or counselors.

A **bachelor's degree** in psychology qualifies a person to assist psychologists and other professionals in community mental health centers, vocational rehabilitation offices, and correctional programs; to work as research or administrative assistants; and to take jobs as trainees in government or business. However, without additional academic training, their advancement opportunities in psychology are severely limited.

In the federal government, candidates having at least 24 semesters hours in psychology and one course in statistics qualify for entry level positions. Competition for these jobs is keen, however. Clinical psychologists generally must have completed the Ph.D. or Psy.D. requirements and have served an internship; vocational and guidance counselors usually need 2 years of graduate study in counseling and 1 year of counseling experience.

In most cases, 2 years of full-time graduate study are needed to earn a master's degree in psychology. Requirements usually include practical experience in an applied setting or a master's thesis based on a research project. A master's degree in school psychology requires about 2 years of course work and a 1-year internship.

Five to 7 years of graduate work usually are required for a doctoral degree. The Ph.D. degree culminates in a dissertation based on original research. Courses in quantitative research methods, which include the use of computers, are an integral part of graduate study and usually necessary to complete the dissertation. The Psy.D. is usually based on practical work and examinations rather than a dissertation. In clinical or counseling psychology, the requirements for the doctoral degree generally include a year or more of internship or supervised experience.

Competition for admission into most graduate programs is keen. Some universities require an undergraduate major in psychology. Others prefer only basic psychology with courses in the biological, physical, and social sciences, statistics, and mathematics.

Most colleges and universities offer a bachelor's degree program in psychology; several hundred offer a master's and/or Ph.D. program. A relatively small number of professional schools of psychology, some affiliated with colleges or universities, offer the Psy.D. The American Psychological Association (APA) presently accredits doctoral training programs in clinical, counseling, and school psychology. The National Council for Accreditation of Teacher Education, with the assistance of the National Association of School Psychologists, is also involved in the accreditation of advanced degree programs in school psychology. APA also accredits institutions that provide internships for doctoral students in school, clinical, and counseling psychology.

Although financial aid is difficult to obtain, some universities award fellowships or scholarships or arrange for part-time employment. The Veterans Administration (VA) offers predoctoral traineeships to interns in VA hospitals, clinics, and related training agencies. The National Science Foundation, the Department of Health and Human Services, and many other organizations also provide grants to psychology departments to help fund student stipends.

Psychologists in independent practice or those who offer any type of patient care, including clinical, counseling, and school psychologists, must meet certification or licensing requirements. All states and the District of Columbia have such requirements. Licensing laws vary by state, but generally require a doctorate in psychology, completion of an approved internship, and 1 to 2 years of professional experience. In addition, most states require that applicants pass an examination. Most state boards administer a standardized test and, in many instances, additional oral or essay examinations. Very few states certify those with a master's degree as psychological assistants or associates. Some states require continuing education for license renewal. Most states require that licensed or certified psychologists limit their practice to those areas in which they have developed professional competence through training and experience.

The American Board of Professional Psychology recognizes professional achievement by awarding diplomas primarily in clinical psychology, clinical neuropsychology, and counseling, forensic, industrial and organizational, and school psychology. Candidates need a doctorate in psychology, 5 years of experience, and professional endorsements; they also must pass an examination.

Even more so than in other occupations, aspiring psychologists who are interested in direct patient care must be emotionally stable, mature, and able to deal effectively with people. Sensitivity, compassion, and the ability to lead and inspire others are particularly important for clinical work and counseling. Research psychologists should be able to do detailed work independently and as part of a team. Verbal and writing skills are necessary to communicate treatment and research findings. Patience and perseverance are vital qualities because results from psychological treatment of patients or research often are long in coming.

What is the Employment Outlook?

Employment of psychologists is expected to grow much faster than the average for all occupations through the year 2005. Largely because of the substantial investment in training required to enter this specialized field, psychologists have a strong attachment to their occupation; only a relatively small proportion leave the profession each year. Nevertheless, replacement needs are expected to account for most job openings, similar to most occupations.

Programs to combat the increase in alcohol abuse, drug dependency, marital strife, family-violence crime, and other problems plaguing society should stimulate employment growth. Other factors spurring demand for psychologists include increased emphasis on mental health maintenance in conjunction with the treatment of physical illness; public concern for the development of human resources, including the growing elderly population; increased testing and counseling of children; and more interest in rehabilitation of prisoners. Changes in the level of government funding for these kinds of services could affect the demand for psychologists.

Job opportunities in health care should remain strong, particularly in health care provided networks, such as health maintenance and preferred provider organizations, that specialize in mental health, and in nursing homes and alcohol and drug abuse rehabilitation programs. Job opportunities will arise in businesses, nonprofit organizations, and research and computer firms. Companies will use psychologists' expertise in survey design, analysis, and research to provide personnel testing, program evaluation, and statistical analysis. The increase in employee assistance programs, in which psychologists help people stop smoking, control weight, or alter other behaviors, also should spur job growth. The expected wave of retirement among college faculty, beginning in the late 1990's, should result in job openings for psychologists in colleges and universities.

Other openings are likely to occur as psychologists study the effectiveness of changes in health, education, military, law enforcement, and consumer protection programs. Psychologists are also increasingly studying the effects on people of technological advances in areas such as agriculture, energy, the conservation and use of natural resources, and industrial and office automation.

Opportunities are best for candidates with a doctoral degree. Persons holding doctorates from leading universities in applied areas such as school, clinical, counseling, health, industrial, and educational psychology should have particularly good prospects. Psychologists with extensive training in quantitative research methods and computer science may have a competitive edge over applicants without this background.

Graduates with a master's degree in psychology may encounter competition for the limited number of jobs for which they qualify. Graduates of master's degree programs in school psychology should have the best job prospects, as schools are expected to increase student counseling and mental health services. Some master's degree holders may find jobs as psychological assistants in community mental health centers; these positions often require direct supervision by a licensed psychologist. Others may find jobs involving research and data collection and analysis in universities, government, or private companies.

Bachelor's degree holders can expect very few opportunities directly related to psychology. Some may find jobs as assistants in rehabilitation centers or in other jobs involving data collection and analysis. Those who meet state certification requirements may become high school psychology teachers.

Earnings. According to a 1991 survey by the American Psychological Association, the median annual-salary of psychologists with a doctoral degree was $48,000 in counseling psychology, $50,000 in research positions, $53,000 in clinical psychology, $55,000 in school psychology, and $76,000 in industrial/organizational psychology. In university psychology departments, median annual salaries ranged from $32,000 for assistant professors to $55,000 for full professors. The median annual salary of master's degree holders was $35,000 for faculty, $37,000 in counseling psychology, $40,000 in clinical psychology, $48,000 in research positions, $50,000 in industrial/organizational psychology, and $52,000 in school psychology. Some psychologist have much higher earning, particularly those in private practice.

The federal government recognizes education and experience in certifying applicants for entry-level positions. In general, the average starting salary for psychologists having a bachelor's degree was about $18,300 a year in 1993; those with superior academic records could begin at $22,800. Clinical psychologists having a Ph.D. or Psy.D degree and 1 year of internship could start at $33,600; some individual could start at $40,300. The average salary for psychologists in the federal government in nonsupervisory, supervisory, and managerial positions was about $54,400 a year in 1993.

Related Occupations. Psychologists are trained to conduct research and teach, evaluate, counsel, and advise individuals and groups with special needs. Other who do this kind of work include psychiatrists, social workers, sociologists, clergy, special education teachers, and counselors.

Sources of Additional Information

- For information on careers, educational requirements, financial assistance, and licensing in all fields of psychology, contact the American Psychological Association, Education in Psychology and Accreditation Offices, Education Directorate, 750 1st Street, NE, Washington, DC 20002.
- For information on careers, educational requirements, and licensing of school psychologists, contact the National Association of School Psychologists, 8455 Colesville Road, Suite 1000, Silver Spring , MD 20910
- Information about state licensing requirement is available from the Association of State and Provincial Psychology Boards, P.O. Box 4389, Montgomery, AL 36109.
- Information on traineeships and fellowships is available from colleges and universities that have graduate departments of psychology.

Graduate education is a process of further refining a general interest in psychology during which students become increasingly more proficient in and knowledgeable of an area of psychological specialization. The following description of 15 of these areas (from APA's Careers in Psychology booklet) will serve as an introduction for students who are pursuing careers that require graduate education in a specialized area of psychology. You will see that you are familiar with many of these categories, but this list goes into more detail than the previous essay did.

Median Salaries For Psychologists with Masters and Doctorates

The employment outlook for psychologists with master's and doctorates is excellent, but is also dependent upon area of specialization. A 1982 survey revealed that less than 1% of all members of APA with doctorates were unemployed, a rate significantly lower than for other similarly prepared social scientists. Opportunities in both the private (i.e., business and industry) and public sectors (i.e., federal, state, and local government agencies) should increase into the 1990s as demand for the expertise of psychologists (e.g., to increase job satisfaction and performance) and support for special groups (e.g., the aged) continues to grow. The future looks particularly promising for those with advanced degrees in clinical, counseling, health, and industrial/organizational psychology. The probability of attaining challenging and rewarding employment with these degrees can be substantially enhanced with supporting education or experience in quantitative research methods and computer applications.

Pion and Bramblett conducted a survey for the American Psychological Association in 1985 to determine the *median* salaries of psychologists with masters and doctoral degrees in a variety of areas of psychological specialization. The following table summarizes their results. Please note that this data is form 1985; if the survey was performed today, the median salaries would be significantly higher.

Area of Employment/Specialization	Master's	Doctorate
Administration of Research	$46,000	$52,000
Industrial/Organizational Psychology	$40,000	$52,000
Educational Administration	$39,000	$44,000
Administration of Human Services	$34,000	$40,000
Research	$31,000	$40,000
Clinical Psychology	$28,000	$40,000
Counseling	$30,000	$33,000
School Psychology	$28,000	$30,000
College/University Faculty	$25,000	$32,000

The results of a more recent study (reported in the September, 1994 issue of Salary Survey) reported that the average *beginning* salary offered to those with a master's degree in psychology was $23,944, and a doctorate in psychology was $43,278.

AREAS OF SPECIALIZATION IN PSYCHOLOGY*

Clinical Psychology

Clinical psychologists assess and treat people with psychological problems. They may act as therapists for people experiencing normal psychological crises (e.g., grief) or for individuals suffering from chronic psychiatric disorders. Some clinical psychologists are generalists who work with a wide variety of populations, while others work with specific groups like children, the elderly, or those with specific disorders (e.g., schizophrenia). They may be found in hospitals, community health centers, or private practice.

*This information is taken verbatim from a pamphlet entitled *Careers in Psychology* published by the American Psychological Association.

Counseling Psychology

Counseling psychologists do many of the same things that clinical psychologists do. However, counseling psychologists tend to focus more on persons with adjustment problems, rather than on persons suffering from severe psychological disorders. Counseling psychologists are employed in academic settings, community mental health centers, and private practice. Recent research tends to indicate that training in counseling and clinical psychology are very similar.

Developmental Psychology

Developmental psychologists study how we develop intellectually, socially, emotionally, and morally during our lifespan. Some focus on just one period of life (e.g., childhood or adolescence). Developmental psychologists usually do research and teach in academic settings, but many act as consultants to day-care centers, schools, or social service agencies.

Experimental Psychology

This area of specialization includes a diverse group of psychologists who do research in the most basic areas of psychology (e.g., learning, memory, attention, cognition, sensation, perception, motivation, and language). Sometimes their research is conducted with animals instead of humans. Most of these psychologists are faculty members at colleges and universities.

Educational Psychology

Educational psychologists are concerned with the study of human learning. They attempt to understand the basic aspects of learning, and then to develop materials and strategies for enhancing the learning process. For example, an educational psychologist might study reading and develop a new technique for teaching reading from the results of the research.

Social Psychology

Social psychologists study how our beliefs, feelings, and behaviors are affected by other persons. Some of the topics of interest to social psychologists are attitudes, aggression, prejudice, love, and interpersonal attraction. Most social psychologists are on the faculty of colleges and universities, but an increasing number are being hired by hospitals, federal agencies, and businesses to perform applied research.

School Psychology

School psychologists are involved in the development of children in educational settings. They are typically involved in the assessment of children and the recommendation of actions to facilitate students' learning. They often act as consultants to parents and administrators to optimize the learning environments of specific students.

Industrial/Organizational Psychology

Industrial/Organizational (I/O) psychologists are primarily concerned with the relationships between people and their work environments. They may develop new ways to increase productivity or be involved in personnel selection. You can find I/O psychologists in businesses, industry, government agencies, and colleges and universities. I/O psychologists are probably the most highly paid psychologists.

Physiological Psychology

Physiological psychology is one of psychology's hottest areas because of the recent dramatic increase in interest in the physiological correlates of behavior. These psychologists study both very basic processes (e.g., how brain cells function) and more observable phenomena (e.g., behavior change as a function of drug use or the biological/genetic roots of psychiatric disorders). Some physiological psychologists continue their education in clinical areas and work with people who have neurological problems.

Environmental Psychology

Environmental psychologists are concerned with the relations between psychological processes and physical environments ranging from homes and offices to urban areas and regions. Environmental psychologists may do research on attitudes toward different environments, personal space, or the effects on productivity of different office designs.

Health Psychology

Health psychologists are concerned with psychology's contributions to the promotion and maintenance of good health and the prevention and treatment of illness. They may design and conduct programs to help individuals stop smoking, lose weight, manage stress, prevent cavities, or stay physically fit. They are employed in hospitals, medical schools, rehabilitation centers, public health agencies, and in private practice.

Family Psychology

Family psychologists are concerned with the prevention of family conflict, the treatment of marital and family problems, and the maintenance of normal family functioning. They design and conduct programs for marital enrichment, pre-marital preparation, and improved parent-child relations. They also conduct research on topics such as child abuse, family communications patterns, and the effects of divorce and remarriage. Family psychologists are often employed in medical schools, hospitals, community agencies, and in private practice.

Rehabilitation Psychology

Rehabilitation psychologists work with people who have suffered physical deprivation or loss at birth or during later development as a result of damage or deterioration of function (e.g., resulting from a stroke). They help people overcome both the psychological and situational barriers to effective functioning in the world. Rehabilitation psychologists work in hospitals, rehabilitation centers, medical schools, and in government rehabilitation agencies.

Psychometrics and Quantitative Psychology

Psychometric and quantitative psychologists are concerned with the methods and techniques used to acquire and apply psychological knowledge. A psychometrist revises old intelligence, personality, and aptitude tests and devises new ones. Quantitative psychologists assist researchers in psychology or other fields to design experiments or interpret their results. Psychometrists and quantitative psychologists are often employed in colleges and universities, testing companies, private research firms, and government agencies.

Psychology and the Law, and Forensic Psychology

Psychology and the law studies legal issues from a psychological perspective (e.g., how juries decide cases) and psychological questions in a legal context (e.g., how jurors assign blame or responsibility for a crime). Forensic psychologists are concerned with the applied and clinical facets of the law such as determining a defendant's competence to stand trial or if an accident victim has suffered physical or neurological damage. Jobs in these areas are in law schools, research organizations, community mental health agencies, and correctional institutions.

In spite of the wide variety of choices available to you, I know that many of you will still approach graduate school with the idea that clinical psychology is the most desirable profession. For some of you, it may indeed be the right choice. For others, however, there are areas that would be a better match. Read the following article with your own academic and personal profile in mind. Can you picture yourself in one of these alternative fields?

ALTERNATIVES TO CLINICAL PSYCHOLOGY
FOR THOSE INTERESTED IN HUMAN SERVICES

The following article, by Janet Matthews of Loyola University in New Orleans, was originally presented as part of a panel discussion at the Southeastern Psychological Association (SEPA) convention on April 1, 1994. It was reprinted in the Fall 1994 issue of the *Psi Chi Newsletter*.

Because of its long history, clinical psychology has often been viewed by undergraduate students as the major career direction for those who are interested in employment in the human services. However, despite the increasing number of available clinical psychology programs, admission rates continue to be rather small. Many of the programs in clinical psychology are highly selective in their admission procedures. It is not unusual for students who have very good credentials to be rejected by the majority of programs to which they apply. It is against this background that the original program at SEPA was organized. This presentation addressed programs in the areas of counseling psychology, professional counseling, marriage and family therapy, physical therapy, occupational therapy, and art therapy. Because of time and space limitations, my comments here are intended to be general in nature and may not apply to a specific program.

Counseling Psychology

Let's start with counseling psychology. Like clinical psychology, these programs require completion of the doctoral degree. These programs are accredited by the American Psychological Association (APA) with new programs being added regularly and previously accredited programs being reviewed on a regular basis. A list of these programs is provided annually in the December issue of the *American Psychologist*. According to the December 1993 issue, there were 63 such programs. Two of these 63 programs (University of California-Santa Barbara; University of Massachusetts) were no longer accepting new students due to their being phased out in favor of an APA-accredited program in combined professional-scientific psychology. A third program (University of North Carolina-Chapel Hill) was just being phased out. Thus, there currently are 60 such choices available to students.

Students from traditional psychology departments tend to notice several things about these counseling programs when they go to the list. One point is the degree offered. Most of these programs culminate in the PhD degree. Three of these programs (Boston University; Columbia University, which also offers the PhD; West Virginia University) offer the EdD degree. Many psychology students are unfamiliar with this degree and do not know whether or not it will lead them to their desired career goals. One program, University of Pittsburgh, offers the PsyD in addition to the PhD in its program. Thus, a starting point in evaluating the suitability of these programs to your needs is to read the program goals and see if they are appropriate for you.

Another point which often confuses students who are reading the description of these programs is the variety of department names where the programs are located. The current list includes:

- department of psychology
- department of psychology and education
- department of counseling and counseling psychology
- department of counseling psychology and guidance services
- department of counseling, developmental psychology, and research methods
- department of developmental studies and counseling
- department of education
- division of psychological and educational services
- department of social, organizational, and counseling psychology
- department of counseling and human development services
- department of counseling
- division of psychological and quantitative foundations
- department of educational psychology and leadership studies
- department of counseling and personnel services
- department of human services and applied behavioral science
- department of educational and psychological studies
- department of counseling, educational psychology, and special education
- division of counseling psychology and counselor education
- department of applied psychology
- division of organizational and psychological studies
- department of applied behavioral studies in education
- psychology in education
- department of counseling, rehabilitation counseling, and counseling psychology

With such an array of department titles, students may begin to wonder whether or if there is a common theme across these programs, and whether or not their background in psychology will prepare them for the coursework required. My experience has been that there is a common thread which is part of the APA accreditation process. Regardless of the department in which the program is located, it must meet the same criteria in order to be accredited by APA. The only way you will know whether or not the program's goals are consistent with your own is to read the program description.

What about admission criteria for these programs? Just like clinical programs, these criteria will vary somewhat by program. Some will be more selective than others. I have found, however, that these programs, as a group, are more likely than clinical programs to place strong emphasis on your practical experience. What does this difference in emphasis mean in terms of your probability of admission? First, if your program offers a field experience in which you can spend time in a mental health facility, you really need to take this course. If your program does not offer this course, then it is important for you to obtain such experience in some other way. One option is to volunteer for such community programs as crisis lines. I tend to advocate this type of experience because it typically provides you with both training prior to beginning work and supervision while you are working. Many of these crisis lines also provide the type of flexible hours which integrate well with students' class schedules. You can often do your volunteer work during evening and weekend hours.

Another option for gaining experience is to obtain either a summer job or part-time work as an aide in a psychiatric hospital. The requirements for these positions vary with the facility and some facilities will require a college degree for employment. If you are planning to take some time away from school between your undergraduate studies and the start of graduate school, such a job could assist you in admission to a counseling psychology program. Keep in mind, however, that these are doctoral programs which are going to require that you conduct research for a thesis and a dissertation, and that they are going to expect quality undergraduate grades and GRE scores for admission. Traditionally, these programs have not been quite as competitive as clinical programs and thus have gained popularity in terms of applications. Advanced students in some of these programs obtain predoctoral internships in clinical settings, and studies have indicated that graduates of many of these programs are indistinguishable from clinical psychologists in terms of their employment settings five years after they graduate.

Professional Counseling

Professional counseling programs are often terminal master's degree programs. They tend to be designed to enable their graduates to obtain a credential as a licensed professional counselor or similar title depending on the state in which they are located. Like counseling psychology programs, they are located in a range of academic departments such as psychology, education, and counselor education. Because of their orientation of training practitioners, they tend to place less emphasis on the "basic science" side of the training, but rather focus on the applied skills their graduates will need to function effectively. Practical experiences, called by such names as "practicum" or "externship," are a major part of the degree program.

What are you trained to do when you complete such a program? The answer to that question will vary somewhat depending on your state of residence and the specific program. In general terms, you may work in a psychiatric facility or in a private practice setting. You probably will need to work in a setting where someone else can qualify for reimbursement from insurance companies. Although you may do some psychological assessment, the nature of this assessment may be limited by the laws of the state. You are most likely to be doing intellectual, educational, and vocational assessments. In terms of therapy, your work may involve individual, couples, family, or group work. Some programs have a specialty focus, such as schools or mental health services, while others are more generic in nature.

Marriage and Family Therapy

Closely related to these counseling programs are the programs which train marriage and family counselors. Some states credential these individuals under the licensed professional counselor provisions while others have a separate credential for marriage and family therapists/counselors. As the name implies, the specialty here is working with dysfunctional relationships. Like the counseling programs, these training programs are offered in a range of departments including home economics.

In the APA publication *Graduate Study in Psychology and Related Fields*, the index uses both the terms "marriage and family" and "marriage and family therapy" to identify programs which might be of interest to students. To illustrate the importance of knowing about the rules of practice for the state in which you may wish to live, note that many of the programs located in California have a specialty track which is designed to meet the state requirements to be licensed as a marriage, family, child counselor (MFCC). This credential is issued by the Board of Behavioral Science Examiners. These specialty master's degrees often require more credit hours than other applied master's degrees in the same department. For example, at Loyola Marymount University in Los Angeles, the MA in general counseling requires 36 units, the MA in alcohol and drug studies require 39 units, while the specialty track leading to the MFCC exam requires 348 units. At California State-Bakersfield, students who are in the MFCC option are required to enroll for two terms in a traineeship setting under the supervision of a licensed professional. This traineeship experience is described as averaging at least 15 hours each week. For students who are planning to try to work while they are in graduate school or have family obligations, it is important to understand the type of time commitments which are required by our chosen program. While some programs offer the doctoral degree in this specialty, the more common type of program in this area seems to be the terminal master's degree.

Physical Therapy

For students who are interested in pursuing a career in physical therapy, it is important that you have a strong interest in the sciences. While the required courses will vary somewhat depending on your specific program, these schools generally want the beginnings of a premed science background. They will expect you to have had lab courses in biology, chemistry, and physics. The competitive ones are also going to require an interview and will be highly selective. Physical therapy is a very "people-oriented" specialty. Physical therapists are most likely to be employed in a hospital or medical center setting. Some physical therapists are also employed in outpatient medical settings. They may be asked to develop individual programs for people who have a range of physical problems and are of any age. Some physical therapists specialize and therefore work with only one age group. For example, they may work in a children's hospital or a department of pediatrics, centering their work with children.

Others may become affiliated full-time with a specific type of program such as chronic pain or rehabilitation following traumatic brain injury. Your graduate work in this discipline teaches you the relevant human anatomy and physiology as well as the physics of the human system in order to remediate its dysfunction. Most physical therapists have a master's degree. This is a master's degree which requires several years of study with an integrated program of courses and practical experiences.

Occupational Therapy

My next area is occupational therapy. I find that this title is often used synonymously with recreational therapy. In some facilities the job description includes occupational and recreational activities. It may even include elements of creative arts therapy such as art therapy and music therapy. There are, however, specialized programs leading to the master's degree in occupational therapy. There is also a national examination leading to certification in occupational therapy after you have completed a certain amount of supervised work experience. The required courses will vary depending upon the program to which you apply, but generally they want a solid liberal arts background. If you plan to focus on work in psychiatric settings, it would be helpful to have completed undergraduate courses in such areas as abnormal psychology and theories of personality.

What do occupational therapists do in the job setting? Let me describe the work of an occupational therapist with whom I worked and perhaps that will give you an idea of whether or not this is a possible career for you. She was employed in a VAMC. She was part of the treatment team for several programs within the department of psychiatry, including an inpatient program and a partial hospitalization program. She provided input on the strengths and weaknesses of patients who were admitted to these programs. She conducted formal evaluations in such settings as the crafts room and recreational activities. Patients were observed not only in terms of the final product they created but also in how they approached the task. She also evaluated how they handled a range of group activities. Her input was valuable in developing individual treatment plans for these patients.

Creative Arts Therapy

To illustrate the relationship of creative arts therapy to occupational therapy, I will briefly make some comments about art therapy. The brochure for the art therapy program at Emporia State University describes this specialty as "a human-service profession that combines elements of art, art education, and psychology to provide opportunities to explore personal potentials and pathologies through visual and verbal expression." Art therapy, as a discipline, is relatively new. The American Art Therapy Association was founded in 1969. Among its activities are the accreditation of master's degree programs in art therapy and the certification of art therapists. Art therapists use their understanding of imagery and symbolism to tap creative potentials in patients. In order to enter most of these programs, you must have a background in both art and psychology. Because art therapists are expected to be versatile, they must have a background in a range of media in addition to some art specialty. Since art therapists also work with emotionally distressed individuals, admission requirements in this field tend to include both abnormal psychology and theories of personality. Other frequently recommended courses are developmental psychology and psychological testing. Art therapy master's degree programs tend to take two years to complete. In order to be accredited by the American Art Therapy Association, they must include at least nine semester hours of internship in addition to practicum experiences.

I hope that this information helps to provide an overview of some of the alternative programs for students interested in careers in human services. Although there are only a limited number of openings in clinical psychology programs, there are a variety of other options and career choices available in related fields, including areas of study in addition to the ones mentioned above.

PREPARING FOR GRADUATE SCHOOL

It is a good idea to make the decision whether or not to attend graduate school early on in your undergraduate career. That way, you can begin developing the skills and characteristics that are necessary for graduate school admission.

You can begin the decision making process with this light-hearted test. I promise that it will be one of the easiest tests that you'll take on the road to grad school admission—but you should actually consider your answers quite carefully as you contemplate your future.

The Unvalidated Graduate School Potential Test

Your answers to the following 22 yes-no questions (modified from Keith-Spiegel, cited in Fretz & Stang, 1988) will give you a good idea of your potential for success in graduate school as determined by your current values and level of motivation. Answer each question honestly and truthfully. This is not a standardized or validated test, and its items are so transparent that anyone can fake them. Unless you are completely honest with yourself, the results will be of no value.

_____ 1. Does the idea of living at near-poverty level for 2-7 years and studying most of the time repulse you?

_____ 2. Do you enjoy writing term papers?

_____ 3. Does the idea of making verbal presentations of academic material in front of a group bother you?

_____ 4. Do you enjoy reading psychology books even if they are not assigned?

_____ 5. Do you put off studying for tests or writing papers as long as possible?

_____ 6. Do you often give up desirable social opportunities in order to study?

_____ 7. Do you want to earn a high salary when you finish graduate school?

_____ 8. Do you like to study?

_____ 9. Do you have trouble concentrating on your studies for hours at a time?

_____ 10. Do you occasionally read recent issues of psychology journals.

_____ 11. Do you dislike library research?

_____ 12. Do you have a drive to enter the profession of psychology?

_____ 13. Are there many other careers, besides being a psychologist, that you would like to pursue?

_____ 14. Do you intend to work full-time at a career?

_____ 15. Are you sick of school right now?

_____ 16. Are your grades mostly A's and B's?

_____ 17. Do you want to stop being a student and start being a real, wage-earning human?

_____ 18. Did you do well (i.e., receive an A or B) in statistics?

_____ 19. Do you feel a Ph.D. is desirable primarily because of the social status it gives to those who hold it?

_____ 20. Do you like doing research?

_____ 21. Do you dislike competing with other students?

_____ 22. Can you carry out projects and study without direction from anyone else?

Give yourself a point for every even-numbered question you answered with a "yes" and for every odd-numbered question you answered with a "no." The higher your score, the higher your potential for success in graduate school.

***

Now, if you passed the test with flying colors, it's time to look a little deeper and begin to evaluate yourself as a potential graduate school candidate. The following survey deals specifically with clinical psychology, but it can serve as a general guideline for other disciplines as well.

Characteristics Of Successful Graduate Students In Clinical Psychology

Why are some graduate students successful and others are not? Pure intellectual abilities—as measured by the GRE and reflected, to a certain extent, in undergraduate GPA—play a significant role, but there is more to graduate school success than raw brain power. Mental toughness, self-reliance, a desire to excel, and a commitment to scholarship are the essential personal characteristics of a student who can adapt to the rigor, stress, and often impersonal nature of graduate school. The successful graduate student is one who possesses both the intellectual abilities and the necessary personal characteristics. Descutner and Thelen (1989) asked 79 faculty members from nine APA-approved clinical psychology graduate programs to describe a successful clinical psychology graduate student by rating 25 characteristics and behaviors on a 6-point scale ranging from not important (1) to very important (6). These characteristics and behaviors (and their average ratings) are listed below in decreasing order of rated importance.

Working hard 5.60
Getting along with people 5.17
Writing ability 4.83
Clinical/counseling skills 4.81
Doing research..4.74
Handling stress 4.72
Discipline..4.64
Good grades...4.61
High intelligence 4.53
Empathy 4.48

Establishing a relationship with a mentor 4.39
Getting along with peers...4.00
Broad knowledge of psychology 4.00
Specialized knowledge in one or two areas of psychology.................3.88
Reflecting program values..3.78
Being liked by faculty..3.69
Creativity 3.67
Obtaining as master's degree as quickly as possible 3.60
Visibility in the department..3.45
Competitiveness 3.29
Relating to professors on a personal level.......................................3.24
Teaching 2.81
Attractive physical appearance 2.53
Serving on student committees 1.95
Serving on department and university committees...........................1.62

It is no surprise that faculty in clinical psychology programs place a premium value on graduate students who work hard, possess good social skills, and write well. However, a surprise does occur with the fourth and fifth items. Most students preparing for graduate education in clinical psychology assume that clinical and counseling skills will be much more valuable to them in graduate school than their ability to perform research. NOT SO! Descutner and Thelen's data clearly indicate that potential clinicians should work equally as hard to develop their research skills--in courses such as experimental psychology, statistics, computer-assisted research, and directed senior research--as they do to develop their clinical and counseling skills. Another interesting finding from this survey is that the ability to handle stress and display discipline are rated as more important to graduate student success than either good grades or high intelligence. Apparently graduate faculty prefer to work with emotionally stable students who can produce consistently above-average work and meet deadlines than with highly intelligent, straight A students who are personally and academically erratic, unorganized, or unpredictable. Undergraduate students who suffer from stress and who have a difficult time managing their academic and personal lives in a disciplined manner can develop the skills to overcome these deficiencies through classes (e.g., Stress Management) or personal counseling.

"In sum, graduate work takes initiative, independence, perseverance, acceptance of responsibility, and a general freedom from emotional conflict and anxiety. The benefits of going to graduate school, especially a top-ranked school, are enormous, but they demand a high price in sweat and anxiety . . . Succeeding in graduate school requires years of single-minded dedication, much energy, individual initiative, and responsible independent study. We wish you well!" (Fretz & Stang, 1988, p. 79-81).

Does the information on these pages make you nervous? If it does, you are a normal undergraduate student who is contemplating graduate school. Take this information as friendly advice--not as an ominous warning--from people who were just like you before they went to graduate school.

Applicant Characteristics Valued By Graduate Programs

A similar study, performed in 1990 by Herbstrith, Mauer, Appleby, considers ideal characteristics of students in a variety of graduate psychology programs This study is based on the assumptions that graduate schools (a) are aware of the characteristics of students who excel in their programs and (b) use the information they gain from letters of recommendation to identify applicants who possess these characteristics. Recommendation forms from the application packages of 143 graduate programs in clinical, experimental, and industrial/organizational psychology were studied. The applicant characteristics that recommenders were requested to rank in grid formats or include in written descriptions were identified, categorized, and arranged in order of relative frequency. The resulting list—consisting of all characteristics requested on at least 10 recommendation forms—describes the characteristics that psychology graduate programs value in their applicants, ranked in descending order of frequency as indicated by the numbers in parenthesis. It is interesting to note that of the 802 total instances of characteristics included in this list, 332 refer to personal characteristics (preceded by P), 264 refer to acquired skills (preceded by S), and 206 refer to intellectual abilities or knowledge (preceded by I). It appears that graduate programs are most interested in learning about the personal characteristics of their potential applicant from recommenders, that they place secondary emphasis on learning about their applicants' acquired skills, and are less interested in learning about their applicants' intellectual abilities or knowledge from recommenders. This appears to be a reasonable conclusion because graduate programs have access to measures of applicants' intellectual abilities (e.g., verbal and mathematical GRE scores and transcripts), knowledge (e.g., psychology GRE scores), and skills (e.g., applicants' application forms and personal statements), but must rely almost exclusively on the personal experience that recommenders have had with applicants to measure their personal characteristics.

1. P - Motivated and hard-working (154)
2. I - High intellectual/scholarly ability (106)
3. S - Research skills (69)
4. P - Emotionally stable and mature (66)
5. S - Writing skills (64)
6. S - Speaking skills (63)
7. S - Teaching skills/potential (49)
8. P - Works well with others (45)
9. I - Creative and original (41)

10. I - Strong knowledge of area of study (29)
11. P - Strong character or integrity (25)
12. S - Special skills (e.g., computer or lab) (19)
13. I - Capable of analytical thought (17)
14. I - Broad general knowledge (13)
15. P - Intellectually independent (12)
16. P - Possesses leadership ability (10)
17. P - Mentally and physically healthy (10)

We have heard from a few professors on the topic of graduate student characteristics—now let's see what a student has to say.

GETTING INTO GRADUATE SCHOOL:
SECRETS OF STANDING OUT IN THE PILE

The following article by Matt Huss (published in the Spring, 1996 issue of the *Psi Chi Newsletter*) was written when he was a graduate student at the University of Nebraska-Lincoln. It provides some very valuable lessons that Matt learned as a result of his ultimately successful acceptance into the graduate school of his choice.

If you are beginning the process of applying to graduate school, you are realizing it's not easy. You are learning schools are looking for GRE scores of 800, GPAs of 4.5 on a 4.0 scale, at least two dozen publications, and a letter of recommendation from Sigmund Freud. Maybe not, but you probably felt as if this were at least close to the truth at times. I had similar thoughts when I was just applying to PhD programs, especially after I didn't get into a school the first time around. As a result of my first-time failure followed by my later success, I learned there were more factors involved in getting into graduate school than grades or GRE scores. I hope what I have learned can help those of you just starting the process.

GRE Scores and Grades

When people speak of the keys to getting into graduate school, GRE scores and grades are usually the focus. They are seen as first-order criteria. They are referred to as first-order criteria because schools often look at these particular aspects of an application first. While this is true—and the importance of such criteria cannot be overemphasized—they are simply screening mechanisms for most schools. Schools have certain minimums or average scores they have found are characteristic of successful students. If programs advertise that their students' average GRE scores are about 650 and their average GPA is 3.75, realize these are only averages. There are students who were accepted with 800s and 4.0s, but there are also students who were accepted with 550s and 3.3 grade point averages.

Depending on the area, a graduate program may receive anywhere from 50 to 500 applications in any given year. Most of these applicants are going to have high GRE scores and good grades or they wouldn't be applying to graduate school. All of these applications are going to be thrown into the pile. As long as your scores are around these averages, you can stay in the running (i.e., you can stay in the pile). The longer you stay in the pile, the better your chances are of getting into the school. If you have the basic credentials, the things that enable you to stick out from the rest of the applicants are going to get you admitted into the program.

Research

One of the best ways to stand out from the rest of the pile is research, research, research! Most graduate programs are at large universities where faculty are under pressure to publish. Prospective applicants who have demonstrated they are capable of undertaking research projects—and have acquired a number of research skills—are very attractive to a program. These are skills faculty members won't have to spend time teaching a new student.

So how do you get involved in research? There are a number of ways. You can begin by looking up your undergraduate professors' names in the literature and seeing what types of things they are interested in, asking other students around the department, or simply going up to your professor and asking. Ask the faculty at your undergraduate institution for help on a research idea you have developed. If you don't have an idea, even a rough one, ask to help your professor with entering data, searching the library for relevant literature, or collecting the data on one of their projects. None of these are glory jobs, but they get your foot in the door. If your professors are unable to help, and you are at an institution with a graduate program, ask one of the graduate students. As a graduate student, I can tell you that I have never turned away an undergraduate who was willing to make my life easier. Again, you may not be involved in the glory-filled aspects of the research, but you will get your foot in the door. After you have learned some of the basics of psychological research, maybe you will progress to analyzing some of the data, helping design the next study, or helping with the writing of a publication. You will learn enough to design and complete your own research project. Remember, the little mundane things can lead to some really great experiences.

Maybe you have contributed enough to a project to submit it to a research conference as a paper or poster. Submitting proposals and attending these professional conferences can be another way of sticking out from the pile. These experience can be invaluable. You may be intimidated initially by the thought of presenting at a conference and speaking in front of a group of people. However, there are student conferences and Psi Chi sessions at the six regional conferences and at the annual meetings of APA. These opportunities may prove to be less anxiety-provoking while still allowing you to get to meet other students (graduate and undergraduate) and professors whose research you are interested in or have read about in your classes. A student who has several conference presentations and a publication or two is definitely going to stand out from the pile. A school is going to perceive you a someone with a number of skills who can make a unique contribution. Conferences can also be sources of the newest research in the field and for information about the program in which you may be interested. Approach faculty or graduate students and ask them about their programs. You may stand out in that pile because a faculty member recognizes your name and can put a face with it. A graduate student may be the best and most honest source of information about a particular program. They know what it is like working with Dr. X and what the expectations are in terms of research and class work. If you can communicate in a personal statement or an interview that you have done your homework, it is going to impress.

Goals and Credentials

Many times professional conferences help with another facet of standing out from the pile. Know your goals and your credentials. It is important that you have a goal in mind when you apply. Graduate school is not an end, but a means to an end. You attend graduate school because there is something you want to do or want to be that requires you get advanced training. It may be as specific as wanting to obtain an academic position at a major university doing research about hormones that influence human mating habits, or you may simply want to be a child psychologist. The more specific it is, the better able you are going to be at communicating your intentions to a program. Having that goal in mind is going to carry you through a lot of long nights filling out phone-book-sized applications and putting up with the garbage that comes along with getting into graduate school. This doesn't mean your goals can't change later, just that you have a solid idea for why you are entering graduate school now.

Knowing what your credentials are is also very helpful. Examine your strengths and weaknesses thinking about what you need to do to stand out. If you are interested in doing clinical work with battered women, then volunteer at a community shelter. If you are considering teaching at a college or university when you finish school, concentrate on getting involved in research if you aren't already. If your GRE scores weren't so hot the first time you took the exam, use one of the many study guides or computer programs for review or attend one of the GRE preparation classes. If you have a great research or clinical experience, make sure you emphasize that in your application. Be aware of the basic skills you have acquired over your life. Accentuating these skills is going to help you stick out from the pile.

Much of what has been discussed can be captured in two very important secrets to getting into graduate school. First, acquire all of the knowledge you can about getting into graduate school or a particular program. Knowledge truly is power. This may mean reading articles about getting into graduate school (hey, good idea), looking through PsycLIT for the names and research interests of certain professors, attending sessions devoted to the topic at professional conferences, asking your own undergraduate professors, and talking to graduate students and faculty from other universities. Do anything you can to find out about the process. Ask the same questions of a number of different people to get a perspective you may have missed. There are a variety of things that have not been touched upon that can be instrumental in helping you stand out.

Secondly, individuals with the ability to propel themselves through all the hard work involved in getting into graduate school are going to stand out. It has been called motivation, enthusiasm, fire in the belly, or (my personal favorite) the eye of the tiger. Students who have the energy to work harder, do more, and get excited about what they are doing are going to be noticed. Professors enjoy working with students who possess an energy and a curiosity about the field. These are the types of students who are always seeking out additional opportunities to get involved. These are the types of students who stick out from the pile. If you are one of these students, then you possess another characteristic that is going to put you ahead.

Though it is becoming more difficult each year to gain admittance into a graduate program, there are a number of things that prospective students can do to increase their chances. Besides getting the best possible grades and doing well on the GRE, students need to work on the things that will make them unique and stand out from the group. The more secrets you learn, the greater your chances.

Success Factors

Graduate school can be a traumatic experience. Many graduate students spend their time complaining about the heavy work load, the uncaring attitudes of faculty, and the constant pressure of being evaluated. These students quickly begin to devalue their graduate education, deny its relevance, and develop strategies that help them to "beat the system" (i.e., merely satisfying degree requirements without engaging in any actual learning). Graduate school for these people is an unpleasant experience to be endured, survived, and forgotten as quickly as possible. What a shame! Another group seems to thrive on their graduate education. According to Bloom and Bell (1979): "These are the few who proceed through the program with the minimum amount of difficulty and a maximum amount of quality performance. They are respected by the faculty, they receive the best financial assistance, they receive accolades, and as a group, they end up with the best employment" (p. 231). These are the graduate school superstars. But what makes them so successful? Bloom and Bell asked 40 of their colleagues (who had earned doctorates from well-known programs around the country) to describe the superstars they had known. The results were amazingly consistent and can be organized into the following five factors.

Visibility. The most often mentioned behavioral characteristic was visibility. Superstars were observed to be physically present in the department, during and often after working hours.

Hard Working. The next most often mentioned quality was that they were hard working. It is important to point out that the superstars were perceived as hard working because faculty actually saw them working hard. Other students may have worked harder, but because they were working hard at home or in the library, they were not perceived to be as hard working as the superstars.

Reflection of Program Values. A consistently mentioned quality was the faculty's perceptions of their professional values. These values were concordant with program values of research and scholarly excellence. Superstars are engaged in ongoing research projects in addition to their MA and PhD theses. Non-superstars did research because it was a degree requirement. Superstars viewed research as an integral part of their discipline and a desirable and worthwhile activity for any professional psychologist. They were curious enough about a problem to want to see data on it. Superstars also recognized the value of having contact with broad areas of psychology, even though their own programs might be highly specialized.

Professor Attachment. From the time they entered graduate school almost all superstars attached themselves to one or two faculty members with whom they continued to work during the course of their training.

Gratification. The final characteristic was that superstars had the ability to make faculty feel worthwhile and rewarded. Typical faculty responses were "early on, they were easy to teach," "they picked up things quickly," "they could receive and use feedback well," "they were not constant complainers," and "they were able to grow into colleague status without taking advantage." In essence, the superstars listened, learned, grew, and produced, which in turn made the faculty member feel worthwhile and rewarded for his/her investment and chosen occupation (p. 231).

Please note that the above characteristics do <u>not</u> include intelligence, excellent grades, or writing ability. Perhaps these qualities are simply assumed to exist in superstars. The lesson to be learned from these findings is that success in graduate school is due to more that just raw brain power. It is also strongly affected by dedication, hard work, loyalty, a willingness to embrace the values of a program, and the ability to make faculty feel worthwhile and rewarded.

A SAMPLE SCHEDULE FOR GRADUATE SCHOOL ADMISSION

As I said, you should think about graduate school early on in your college career—the earlier you make up your mind, the better off you will be as you approach the application process. There are things that you can begin doing as early as sophomore year to ensure that you give yourself the best chance possible to get in.

The following article by Susan Schumacher (published in the Fall, 1994 issue of the *Psi Chi Newsletter*) provides a timetable of things to do while in college to ensure graduate school acceptance or employment. Post a copy of this article in an obvious place and write the date of completion beside activities as you complete them.

Sophomore Year

- Talk with your teachers who conduct research and/or clinical activities of interest to you and discuss the possibility of becoming involved in these activities with them.

- Attend psychology-related seminars at your school and surrounding institutions and document your attendance. Join the Psi Chi chapter or psychology club on your campus.

- Find out what psychology conferences are held in your region that students can attend. Check the *American Psychologist* (found in your school library or in a psychology faculty member's office) or the *Psi Chi Newsletter* for the locations and dates (usually in the spring), and attend as many as possible.

- Talk to graduate students on your campus and on other campuses (preferably students in the field of psychology) or to those at the meetings in item #3 about graduate school life, finances, and work loads. In addition, ask them about psychology-related seminars or meetings they might be aware of (see items #2 and #3 above).

- Order the APA publication *Preparing for Graduate Study in Psychology: Not for Seniors Only!* Locate a copy of *Getting In: A Step-by-Step Plan for Gaining Admission to Graduate School in Psychology.* Read them!

- Maintain a grade of "B" or better in all psychology courses. This will greatly enhance your chances of graduate school acceptance or employment in the field of psychology. While maintaining this level of performance, do not lose sight of the goal of obtaining knowledge through your courses, research, volunteer activities, contacts with faculty, and meetings you attend.

Junior Year

- Become involved in a research project as part of a course requirement, do an independent study project, or work with a faculty member on his/her research.

- Write a resume as described in the APA publication *Preparing for Graduate Study in Psychology; Not for Seniors Only!* Follow the suggested guidelines, even if the resume is to be submitted to potential employers and not to graduate schools. Emphasize psychology-related extracurricular activities (e.g., meetings and volunteer work). If you are a minority student, emphasize your ethnic identification; it will be to your advantage because of the shortage of minority psychologists and because there are additional sources of financial assistance for minority students.

- Obtain experience through volunteer work if you are interested in clinical or counseling psychology. If possible, do some research in connection with your volunteer activities.

- Submit your research to a student conference and continue item #4 from sophomore year.

- Investigate summer jobs or educational/research opportunities related to psychology. Many summer internships are available through laboratories or professional organizations. If you are a minority student, investigate the minority summer programs, such as those at the University of South Carolina and the University of Georgia, or the minority summer research experience offered by Bell Laboratories. Check with your department faculty on a regular basis concerning available opportunities, and **apply early.**

- Prepare, register for and, in the spring, take the aptitude test of the Graduate Record Examination (GRE) and the Miller Analogies Test (MAT), even if you have not yet decided to apply for graduate school.

- Check with the campus placement office for dates of on-campus visits by recruiters and with your department chair for dates of visits by graduate school representatives. Determine the types of opportunities available and list the ones of greatest interest to you for future contact.

Summer Before Your Senior Year

- Obtain summer employment, experience, or education related to psychology. If you are seriously considering graduate school, retake in summer school any courses in which you received a grade below a "B." Of special importance are Statistics and Research Methods or Experimental Methodology.

- Decide if you are going to graduate school (and, if so, in what field) or if you plan to work immediately following graduation. However, do not do anything that would prevent you from changing your decision later or from pursuing the other option if existing plans fail. The books mentioned in item #3 below should aid you in your decision.

- Consult the APA publication *Graduate Studies in Psychology* for requirements and information on graduate programs in psychology. List schools of interest to you, and request from them bulletins, brochures, financial aid forms, and department application forms. For job ideas, descriptions, skills needed, and interview techniques, consult the following APA publications: *The Psychology Major: Training and Employment Strategies, Getting In: A Step-by-Step Plan for Gaining Admission to Graduate School in Psychology, Career Opportunities for Psychologists.* List job areas to pursue and investigate sources of additional training you will need.

- Prepare for the advanced GRE test in psychology by studying the commercially available books and software, and by re-reading your general psychology textbook, including the sections on statistics and methodology. Register for the early fall offerings of the aptitude and the advanced tests. Repeated testing should improve your scores. Also, register for the Miller Analogies Test (MAT) and study the types of items it contains.

- Revise and update your resume to include new experiences. Remember neatness and organization create a good first impression.

- Save money for graduate school application fees, resumes, and transcript costs.

Fall Semester Of Your Senior Year

- Be sure you take (and pass) all courses needed to graduate. Obtain a statement of standing from your registrar to verify this. You don't want any surprises next semester when you apply for graduation!

- Discuss with your advisor and other psychology faculty members the graduate programs or jobs of interest to you. Show them your resume so they may better counsel you and determine if your expectations are realistic, and obtain a list of additional suggestions from them. Discuss the performance of other students from your department in the graduate programs or business settings of potential interest to you. Also discuss the socioeconomic conditions that might affect you at the schools, industries, clinics, or hospitals in which you are interested, and in the regions or cities in which they are located.

- If possible, actually visit the schools, industries, or agencies of greatest interest, and establish personal contact with key people at each. Obtain impressions of the institution or organization from others having similar backgrounds and qualifications. Even if there are no existing vacancies, the expression of interest and establishment of personal contact will give you an added advantage should a vacancy occur.

- Prepare for and take the aptitude and advanced tests of the GRE in October if possible, and no later than December. Also take the MAT.

- Register to take the advanced test again in December, or January at the latest. Note the possibility that the January test date may be too late for your scores to be considered for fellowships at some institutions.

- Obtain information on available fellowships, scholarships, assistantships, and loans not associated with the institutions to which you plan to apply. Obtain this information from your financial aid office.

- Request a student copy of your transcript from every institution you have attended and check for errors. This process may take longer than you think, especially if there are errors, so allow ample time.

- Duplicate your resume and transcripts for distribution. If you plan to apply to graduate school, remember there are application fees (which may be waived, so ask) and charges for mailing official transcripts (which should follow as soon as the fall semester's grades are included). Even resume duplications and mailing can be expensive for a student budget.

- Check the latest copy of *Graduate Study in Psychology* to obtain requirements and deadlines for various graduate school applications and fellowships. Check the campus placement office for dates of visiting recruiters who will conduct job interviews on campus. Follow through on these early.

- Write to the personnel office of the states in which you wish to apply for jobs, and request descriptions of positions related to psychology. If you need to take the civil service or other exams to qualify for these positions, register for the required exams. Put your name on mailing lists for job announcements.

- Narrow down your list of schools to approximately ten, including at least two where you are confident you will be accepted. If you are job-oriented or are uncertain you will be accepted into any graduate program, list in order of preference the types of jobs, and if possible, the specific agencies with whom you would consider accepting employment. Remember, both job and admission competition are keen, and you may not be able to obtain your first or second choice. Be prepared to be flexible. Post any deadlines for application where you will constantly see them.

- Determine from whom you wish to obtain letters of recommendation, and notify these people at least three weeks before the deadline for your application. Supply them with necessary forms, addresses, information about your qualifications and due dates, along with jobs or programs for which you are applying. Include a stamped addressed (neatly typed, not hand-written) envelope to each school or agency they must write. Follow up one week before each deadline with a thank-you note (a "friendly" reminder to ensure that your information has been sent).

- Request that your GRE and MAT scores be sent to all schools or employers requiring them. If your scores are high and will be considered an asset, mail them to all places you are applying. Request that transcripts be mailed to all schools and agencies.

- Check before Christmas to be certain all materials, especially recommendations, have been sent. Most incomplete applications result from missing letters of recommendation. Be persistent.

- Include in your application package to graduate schools or employers all requested materials, a resume, copies of transcripts and test scores, and names of those sending recommendations. Indicate what additional material is to follow (transcripts with your fall grades, revised test scores, etc.). **Follow application instructions exactly.** For job seekers, contact local community service agencies, hospitals, research institutes, public relations firms, test or survey developers, and market research departments. Send them letters of inquiry for position vacancies and a summary of your credentials. Make these contacts as personal as possible. Keep a record of all contacts made and all materials sent to each employer or school.

Spring Semester Of Your Senior Year

- Verify in January that all you application materials were received at every place you applied.

- Send additional GRE results (if higher) and fall semester grade report to update your applications.

- Expect first choice offers to be made by graduate schools before April 1; however, vacancies may occur any time prior to the fall semester, due to changes in plans of those already accepted. If you have not been accepted anywhere by April 15 you should:

- Call everywhere you applied, asking them to keep your application active through the summer, as you are still interested, even in a last-minute acceptance.

- Call admissions offices of schools whose requirements you easily meet, but to which you did not apply, to see if they are still considering applicants. If so, apply.

- Check *Graduate Study in Psychology* for schools with late or no deadlines and apply.

- If you are rejected by doctoral programs, apply to master's programs with late or open admission dates.

- Job hunt, using the guidelines given above. You may need to postpone graduate school for a year and reapply. A good job related to psychology will enhance your credentials.

- Contact psychology faculty whom you have met from other institutions, and request their advice (i.e., keep your network lines open).

- Follow up with a phone call or letter on job applications submitted, and continue to make as many contacts with agencies and industries as possible. Often "word-of-mouth" among personnel managers results in unexpected employment.

- Keep your most important psychology textbooks. They will come in handy later, whether in graduate school or on the job.

If you were not accepted into a graduate school, after checking all institutions for last minute openings and applying to several master's degree programs, don't give up! Seek employment, preferably related to psychology, and try to be admitted as a special graduate student at the nearest institution offering graduate courses in psychology. Enroll in one or two courses per semester that won't conflict with your work schedule and **commit yourself to making an "A"** in these courses. The more experimentally oriented the course, the better (an "A" in graduate statistics will be quite valuable in convincing evaluation committees to ignore a "C" in undergraduate statistics). When you reapply to graduate school next year, these efforts will assist in persuading the review committee that you are persistent, capable of performing at the graduate level, and motivated to continue to study in psychology. These graduate credits may be transferred later toward a degree. You may even seek at midterm to be admitted to the graduate program in psychology where you are taking the graduate work (although you may still wish to transfer to another program later). But, to reap these benefits, **you must perform well in any graduate courses you attempt!** If you cannot take graduate courses, repeat any relevant undergraduate courses in which you received a grade lower than "B." Mention in future applications your revised GPA, as it will not be reflected on your original undergraduate transcript. You should then update your resume, correcting weaknesses if possible. Review those places to which you applied the previous spring, realistically determining why you were rejected, and reapply to those for which you feel you are qualified. You may have been rejected because the particular applicants against whom you were compared were all exceptional; the next year this may not happen. Apply to a few new places, too. Follow the senior year timetable again, and consider retaking the GRE and MAT if your scores were low. Save what money you can while working so the availability of financial aid will not dictate if you are able to attend graduate school.

APPLYING TO GRADUATE SCHOOL

If you follow a schedule similar to the one on the previous pages, the actual application should not be a cause for panic. It is, of course, very important—be sure to allow yourself plenty of time for every aspect of it. The GREs, the personal statement, the curriculum vitae, and gathering good letters of recommendation—all of these take time and energy, but the payback can be enormous when you receive a letter of acceptance in the mail.

In this section, we will hear from a few experts on the various components of the application and then I will give you some concrete examples of what these experts are talking about.

Graduate School Admission Criteria

(This article is an edited version of a paper presented by Karen Ford at the 1994 American Psychological Society convention and reprinted in the Fall, 1994 edition of the *Psi Chi Newsletter*.)

I would like to discuss the relative importance of some graduate admissions criteria, specifically, undergraduate coursework, research experience, clinical experience, GRE scores, and undergraduate GPA.

Undergraduate Coursework. Most graduate programs in psychology require or prefer the equivalent of a major or minor in psychology. Furthermore, the faculty in these programs prefer that the student receives a broad background in the principles of psychology and is exposed to a broad range of context areas. They tend to prefer that students wait until graduate school to "specialize" in clinical or counseling or developmental, etc.

Courses outside the psychology major in math and science are also desirable. Even for most clinical psychology programs, graduate selection committees are biased toward scientific and mathematical courses. In accord with this bias is the fact that the majority of graduate programs in clinical, counseling, and experimental require or recommend the statistics course. Experimental and clinical graduate programs also tend to regard the experimental psychology course and a psychology laboratory course as very important.

Experimental graduate programs tend to rank statistics, experimental, and learning as the most important undergraduate courses. Clinical and counseling graduate programs tend to rank statistics, abnormal, experimental, personality, developmental, testing, and learning, in that order, as most important. Educational graduate programs rank statistics, developmental, testing, experimental, abnormal, and personality, in that order, as most important. If you already know the graduate programs to which you are interested in applying, you can check the admission requirements of those specific programs in APA's most recent *Graduate Study in Psychology and Associated Fields*.

The ideal undergraduate program in psychology should require statistics, courses in introductory and experimental psychology, and at least one or two laboratory courses. However, undergraduate coursework is not the primary basis for decisions about admittance to graduate school; letters of recommendation, GPA, GRE scores, and research experience are probably more important than undergraduate coursework.

Undergraduate GPA. Graduate programs in counseling tend to put more importance on GPA based on the last two years of undergraduate work than overall GPA. Counseling programs also tend to value previous graduate work as a plus. This is not so for experimental and clinical programs. Selection committees for these graduate programs look at overall GPA and usually prefer students without any previous graduate training.

Research And Clinical Experience. Most clinical and experimental graduate programs regard research experience as very important, whereas counseling programs place more importance on clinical experience. Undergraduates who have presented a paper at a convention or published a journal article stand out among the many applicants to graduate programs. However, it is common for graduate school applicants to list clinical fieldwork or practicum experience, so inclusions of that type will not necessarily help you stand out as an applicant. It is generally expected for applicants to clinical or counseling programs to have clinically related experience.

Graduate Record Exam. The Graduate Record Exam (GRE) is required by virtually every graduate program in psychology. It consists of two separate three hour tests: (a) the General Test (composed of sections measuring verbal, quantitative, and analytical abilities) and (b) a Subject Test that measures understanding of basic psychological principles and facts. Most graduate programs require only the General Test, and the verbal and mathematical scores of the General Test are commonly viewed as most important. Consult APA's Graduate Study in Psychology and Associated Fields to determine the specific requirements of individual programs. The GRE is administered at Butler University five times a year--in October, December, February, April, and June (General Test only). Students should obtain a copy of the GRE Information Bulletin (that contains an application form and sample test questions) from the Registrar's office during their junior year. Registration deadlines are usually six weeks before each test.

Students often ask if it is possible to study for the GRE. The answer is YES! There are two major reasons for this emphatic response, one dealing with knowledge enhancement and the other with anxiety reduction. There are several published study guides for the GRE (the one published by Barrons is highly recommended) and the psychology department also has a computerized study guide entitled "Mastering the GRE" available in the computer lab. These guides contain sample tests and are designed primarily to prepare a student to take the quantitative and verbal sections of the General Test. Students who intend to go to graduate school should purchase a GRE study guide in their junior year and spend a number of serious hours studying it during the subsequent summer. Re-reading lecture notes from psychology classes and reviewing a copy of a recently published general psychology text book are the best ways to prepare for the GRE Subject Test in psychology. Even if a student does not learn anything new while studying for the GRE (which is highly unlikely), the process of becoming familiar with the type of material to be tested and the format of the test itself will reduce test anxiety and increase test-taking speed. In their chapter from Is Psychology the Major for You?, Lunneborg and Wilson (1987) make the following points about the importance of the GRE and the attitude that students should develop toward it.

"How important is the GRE? Most clinical and experimental graduate programs regard the quantitative and verbal sections of the GRE as very important. The analytical psychology subtests are generally viewed as less important than the other two. Counseling programs tend to regard the GRE scores as moderately, rather than very, important. One's attitude toward the GRE should be acknowledging its importance, studying hard for it, doing as well as possible, and then following through with an application strategy consistent with one's test scores. Poorer-than-expected test scores may mean toning down one's list of prospective graduate programs. In addition, the GRE should be viewed as a one-time endeavor. Even though the test can be retaken, all scores are reported, and the first scores are generally considered as the most valid. There is a 50-50 chance for getting a poorer second score; most students we have known did not do significantly better on a second try" (p. 92).

A recent analysis of students admitted to graduate programs found that for master's programs, the average GRE-Verbal score is 540 and the average GRE-Q score is about 530. For doctoral programs, the average GRE-V score is 604 and the average GRE-Q score is just under 600 (597 or 598). Again, if you know the graduate schools to which you would like to apply, you can check the current Graduate Study in Psychology and Associated Fields for the schools' required and preferred GRE scores.

Note: Another test required by approximately 25% of graduate programs is the Miller Analogies Test (MAT) which consists of 100 analogies administered in 50 minutes. A free booklet describing the MAT can be obtained from the Psychological Corporation, 304 East 85th Street, New York, NY 10017.

The Application

Coursework, your GPA, and your GRE scores—when you sit down to prepare your application, all of these things will already be established. After doing such a large volume of work, you owe it to yourself to put your all into your application. The personal statement is the section of the application that allows for the most creativity—and that deserves the greatest amount of time.

The Personal Statement

Most graduate schools require a personal statement as a part of your application. This statement is often centered around your interest in psychology, your personal background, the reasons you are applying to that particular graduate program, and your career and personable objectives. Although a well-written personal statement will not overcome poor grades or low GRE scores, a poor one will surely hurt your chances of acceptance. Fretz and Stang (1988) cite the following example.

"Take the case of the student with a competitive grade point average and good references who was not accepted to any of the 11 programs he applied for. One cannot be sure, but the biographical statement included with his applications is the suspected reason. First, it was poorly typed, with many smears and crossed-out words. The spelling and grammar were both appalling. Finally, the content left much to be desired. It was far too long--about 15 pages--and went into detail about this person's philosophy of life (which was far from the establishment viewpoint). It also stressed emotional agonies and turning points in his life. Hoping to cure the world of all its evils, this person tried to indicate how a PhD in psychology was necessary to fulfill that end. In short, it was an overstated, ill-conceived essay that may have be been received so badly that it overshadowed his other attributes and data" (p. 45).

Plan and produce your personal statement as carefully as you would a crucial term paper. The following tips (quotes taken from Fretz & Stang) will help you produce a personal statement as impressive and effective as the sample on the following page.

- Word-process your personal statement. It will require a series of drafts, and the inconvenience of rewriting each draft with a conventional typewriter can make you willing to settle for a less-than-perfect final product.

- Before you begin your statement for each school, read as much about their program as possible so that you can tailor your statement to the program and convince the admissions committee that you will fit their program like a glove. "Each year many applicants will write, for example, that they want to attend the counseling psychology program at University X because they want to learn how to counsel emotionally handicapped children--even though the program specifies in its brochure that is does not provide training for work with young children. The selection committee immediately rejects those candidates."

- Prepare an outline of the topics you want to cover (e.g., professional objectives and personal background) and list supporting material under each main topic. Write a rough draft in which you transform your outline into prose. Set it aside and read it a week later. If it still sounds good, go to the next stage. If not, rewrite it until it sounds right.

- Check your spelling, grammar, punctuation, and capitalization carefully. Nothing detracts from the contents of a statement more than these types of errors. Avoid slang words that make you sound uneducated, and overly elaborate words or stilted language that will make you appear pompous or pretentious.

- Ask two of your teachers to read your first rough draft and make suggestions. Incorporate these suggestions into your second rough draft. Ask for another reading and set of suggestions, and then prepare your final statement.

- Your final statement should be as brief as possible--two double-spaced pages are sufficient. Stick to the points requested by each program, and avoid lengthy personal or philosophical discussions. If your statement sounds egocentric or boring, those who read it will assume you are egocentric or boring.

- Do not feel bad if you do not have a great deal of experience in psychology to write about; no one who is about to graduate from college does! Do explain your relevant experiences (e.g., Co-op jobs or research projects), but do not try to turn them into events of cosmic proportion. "Be honest, sincere, and objective--that is the only way to impress the evaluators that you are a person who is already taking a mature approach to life."

A SAMPLE PERSONAL STATEMENT

(This personal statement was written by a student applying to a clinical psychology program.)

I became initially interested in psychology when I was helping a friend who was having problems at home and was considering suicide. I felt so helpless trying to deal with his problems that I decided to learn more about human behavior and how to help those in need. This experience led me to enroll in an introductory psychology course in order to understand more about what motivates people. I have become more and more interested in the field of clinical psychology during my four years at Marian College.

In addition to my educational experience at Marian, I actively pursued work experience in psychology-related fields. I worked for Marian as a resident assistant in one of the dormitories during my junior year. In this role, I encountered students who had problems relating to their family, depression, suicide, alcohol, and drugs. I attained a Co-op position during my senior year as a residential supervisor at the Indianapolis Center for Neuropsychological Rehabilitation, a facility dedicated to teaching brain injured individuals not only to deal with their handicaps, but to overcome them. I witnessed counseling of both clients and their families, and I learned to administer and score several psychological tests used in clinical assessment (e.g., the Wechsler Memory Scale and the MMPI). My work experience has proven to me how much more I need to learn before I can attain my goal of becoming an accomplished researcher and teacher.

I became interested in research as a sophomore when I enrolled in a senior level research class (i.e., Computer-Assisted Research). By the time I graduate, I will have presented a total of five papers on a variety of topics at undergraduate research conferences. My experience with the first study, an examination of mood effects on time perception, led to other research endeavors on topics including student evaluation of faculty, academic integrity, and comparisons of personality profiles of brain injured individuals. The relevance of two of these projects, academic honesty and student evaluation of faculty, led Dr. Louis Gatto, President of Marian College, to invite me to present my results at two Open College Forums. This is the first time a student has presented at an Open College Forum. At St. Louis University, I am specifically interested in the research efforts of Harvey Austrin (hypnosis), Nancy Brown (child adolescent psychotherapy outcomes), and Thomas Grisso (clinical, personality, and community assessment). As an undergraduate, I have learned the importance of working closely with members of the faculty. A great deal can be accomplished by working with someone who is already an expert in the field.

I have become firmly committed to the beliefs that the most appropriate way to answer "real world" questions is through basic research and that these answers should be communicated in a professional manner to those audiences who can benefit most from them. My undergraduate experiences have inspired me to continue my education in graduate school so I can further my research and make a meaningful contribution to the field of psychology.

This applicant is currently a doctoral student in clinical psychology at Purdue. Please note how he stressed the reasons for his interest in clinical psychology, his research experience, and how clearly and honestly he described his undergraduate accomplishments and future goals without assuming a tone of egotistic superiority or false modesty.

The personal statement is your chance to speak directly to the admissions committee, to give them a sense of who you are and what is important to you. You won't be able, however, to get across all of the hard work and exciting experiences that you will have had by the end of your four years in college. The curriculum vitae provides you with the opportunity to share your achievements in a succinct and organized fashion.

The Curriculum Vitae

The word "resume" is seldom used in academic circles. The self-describing document that academic psychologists prepare when they are seeking jobs or representing themselves to their professional colleagues is called a "curriculum vita," which is often shortened to the single word "vita." (Vita is the Latin word for life, and a curriculum vita is a written record of a person's educational life.) The vita is an important part of the application to graduate school. It is also the means of representing oneself in the academic world as a whole

A vita differs from a resume in its emphasis on educational, rather than occupational, experiences and strengths. Students who are planning to go to graduate school should become familiar with the vita-writing process so that they can produce an impressive vita to accompany their graduate school applications. The article that appears on the following pages (taken from the May, 1989 issues of the <u>APS Observer</u>) should help students understand the concept of a vita. It describes, explains, and give examples of the following sections of a well-prepared vita and offers advice that a vita-writer should heed.

Sections Of A Vita

Personal history	Professional positions
Educational history	Professional activities
Membership in professional organizations	Grants
Editorial activities	Papers presented
Papers currently under submission	Statement of professional interest
Publications	Projects underway
Professional references	

General Considerations
Form and style
Detail
What not to include
Padding
Vita development

A SAMPLE CURRICULUM VITAE

MELISSA R. JOHNSON

School Address
Marian College
3200 Cold Spring Road
Indianapolis, IN 46222
Phone: 929-0678

Home Address
154 Springdale Avenue
Plainfield, IN 46789
Phone: 317-897-2641
After May 10, 1996

EDUCATIONAL OBJECTIVE: To obtain a Ph.D. in Counseling Psychology.

CAREER OBJECTIVE: To work with substance-abusing adolescents.

EDUCATION: Bachelor of Arts, Marian College (expected 5/96).
Major: Psychology, Minor: Biology.
Cumulative overall GPA (4.00 scale): 3.35, GPA in psychology classes: 3.80.

GRE SCORES: Verbal 640, Quantitative 610.

HONORS: Elected to Psi Chi (Spring, 1993).
Marian College Honors Program (Fall, 1993 to present).
Dean's List (4 of 6 semesters).

RESEARCH EXPERIENCE:
Collected and analyzed data from the Myers-Briggs personality inventory.
Designed and carried out a research project on academic advising.
Research projects supervised by Dr. Joseph Hingtgen.

TEACHING EXPERIENCE:
Served as a Teaching Assistant in General Psychology (Fall, 1995).
Teaching supervised by Dr. Drew Appleby.

WORK EXPERIENCE:
Behavioral Technician, St. Vincent Stress Center (August, 1994 - present).
Supervised by Dr. Thomas Anderson.
Volunteer, HELP Crisis Center (January 1993 - present).
Supervised by Dr. Joan Elway.

(continued)

PAPERS PRESENTED:

Johnson, M. R., & Plascak-Craig, F. D. (1995, April). <u>Myers-Briggs scores can predict roommate compatibility</u>. Paper presented at the Mid-America Undergraduate Psychology Research Conference, Evansville, IN.

Johnson, M. R., & Plascak-Craig, F. D. (1996, April). <u>Factors affecting the success of academic advising</u>. Paper submitted for presentation at the meeting of the Midwestern Psychological Association.

REFERENCES:

Dr. Drew Appleby
Marian College
3200 Cold Spring Road
Indianapolis, IN 46222

Dr. Faye Plascak-Craig
Marian College
3200 Cold Spring Road
Indianapolis, IN 46222

Dr. Thomas Anderson
St. Vincent Stress Center
7890 Harcourt Road
Indianapolis, IN 46789

Dr. Joan Elway
HELP Crisis Center
2876 North College Street
Indianapolis, IN 47223

The Letter of Recommendation

The personal statement and the vita give you the opportunity to describe yourself. Unfortunately, no admissions committee is going to be willing to take your word alone! The letter of recommendation is the means by which a university is able to get a feeling for the ways that you interact in a classroom setting, and to get the opinion of a professional in the field of psychology.

Strategies for Obtaining Strong Letters of Recommendation. Most graduate programs and potential employers require a minimum of three letters of recommendation as part of their application process. Many provide applicants with forms for recommenders to complete, although a few simply request letters. Choosing those who will recommend you is a crucial process that you should base on the following criteria.

How well do they know you? Almost every recommendation form begins by asking how long and in what capacity the recommender has known the applicant. You will want to choose recommenders who have known you for at least two years and from whom you have taken several classes or worked with on research or departmental projects. Admissions committees and personnel directors are not impressed with recommendations from persons who do not know you well. They make the assumption that either you have done nothing to allow your teachers/adviser to know you well or that those who know you well do not think highly enough of you to write you a letter of recommendation. Do <u>not</u> allow them to make these assumptions about you!

How positively can they recommend you? Do not simply ask faculty members if they will write you letters of recommendation. Ask them if they will write <u>strong</u> letters of recommendation for you. A mediocre letter of recommendation is a death sentence to job or graduate school application. You may have good grades, strong GRE scores, and a creative personal statement, but if one of your carefully selected recommenders writes a letter that paints a weak picture of your potential for success, no graduate school or potential employer will want to take a chance on you. Work hard to give faculty reasons to write you strong letters; then do everything in your power to help them do just that.

How impressed will a graduate admissions committee or potential employer be with your recommenders? Do not ask for letters of recommendation from your family members, high school counselor, physician, or priest/minister/rabbi. They may be able to describe many of your strong personal qualities (e.g., loving, concerned, healthy, and devout), but these qualities are <u>not</u> those about which a graduate admissions committee or potential employer is primarily concerned. Graduate faculty are evaluated by the quality and quantity of their research publications and employers' success is measured by their productivity; they will be looking for students who will help them in their efforts to achieve success. Choose recommenders with whom you have been involved in research, who have instructed research-oriented courses you have taken (e.g., Statistics, Experimental Psychology, and Directed Research), or who can vouch for your initiative, persistence, and creativity. These are the people who can write positively about what you have done or about your potential as a successful future scholar/researcher or employee.

A standard recommendation form is included in this chapter for students contemplating graduate school. Study it carefully to discover the knowledge, skills, and personal characteristics that your recommenders will use to evaluate you; it is never too early to begin to develop them. Many students wait until they are seniors before they begin to think about letters of recommendation and, when they discover that they do not possess the necessary qualities, they bemoan the fact that "nobody ever told me these things would be important!" Do <u>not</u> let this happen to you!

You may wish to compare the information requested on the graduate school recommendation form with the example of the completed "Information for Letters of Recommendation and Resumes" section of the microcomputer advising program contained in this chapter. You will be making great progress towards receiving strong letters of recommendation if you familiarize yourself with this program, do things that will allow you to fill it with impressive information, and up-date it every semester.

SAMPLE LETTER OF RECOMMENDATION

Graduate Admissions Committee
Department of Family Therapy
University of Connecticut
Storrs, CT 06268

Dear Madam or Sir:

I have known <u>Sarah Holmes</u> since she enrolled as a freshman at Marian three and a half years ago. During that time I have come to know her very well as her academic advisor and teacher in four classes. I would like to recommend her to you as a candidate for your graduate program for the following reasons.

<u>Sarah is a very intelligent and motivated young person.</u> She earned a grade of "A" in each of the three classes she has had with me (General Psychology, Developmental Psychology, and Readings in Psychology) and she is performing equally well in the class she is taking from me now (History and Systems of Psychology). She is the type of student who is a pleasure to have in class. It is obvious that she is prepared and ready to participate when she walks through the door, and she retains the same eager attitude and zest until the end of the class. I want to emphasize the word eager; Sarah enjoys learning and cannot seem to get enough of it. This extremely positive attitude will serve her well in graduate school and will motivate her to continue learning throughout her career as a professional psychologist.

<u>She is not only an enthusiastic student, but also a skillful one.</u> I am including a copy of the syllabus from my Readings in Psychology class (our senior capstone class) so that you can know the skills (e.g., critical thinking, computer literacy, library search, and oral and written communication) that she acquired during her first three undergraduate years and mastered as a senior. We have found that this course provides an excellent preparation for the rigors of graduate school. Anyone who earns an "A" in this class--as Sarah did-- is <u>ready</u> for graduate school.

Sarah is an absolutely avid researcher. She is currently involved in two simultaneous research projects, one with me and the other with one of my part-time faculty who holds a full-time position in the Department of Psychiatric Research at the Indiana University Medical School. Both are major projects with potentially significant and publishable results. One deals with the effects of in-house "jobs" on the cognitive status of nursing home residents and the other with the construction of an objective test instrument to measure the intellectual level of college students (according to William Perry's model). Sarah has demonstrated that she can perform these projects in an independent and responsible manner with a minimum of supervision. She is careful to understand the expectations of her research supervisor and then carries out the details of the project in a completely dependable manner. She is precisely the type of student I want as a research assistant.

(continued)

In conclusion, I recommend Sarah to you very highly as a candidate for admission to your graduate program. She is exactly the type of undergraduate I would admit to a graduate program of your type if I was in the position to do so.

Sincerely,

Drew C. Appleby, Ph.D.
Professor and Chairman

Strategies for Receiving Weak Letters of Recommendation (or, what not to do!).
Following this set of rules (modified from a list compiled by Nish and cited in Bloomquist, 1981) will guarantee that you DO NOT receive strong letters of recommendation from your adviser and teachers. Do not allow the sarcastic tone of these rules to interfere with your understanding of their basic message: You cannot expect your teachers and adviser to write you good letters of recommendation if you do not treat them with courtesy and respect.

- Treat your teachers and classes as though you are barely able to tolerate them. An attitude of superior aloofness will show everyone how important you are and how lucky they are to exist at the same time and on the same planet as you.
- Be consistently late to class and other appointments. This will show your teachers how much busier you are than they are.
- Be very casual about class attendance. When you see your teacher after you have missed his class, ask "Did you say anything important in class today?" Act as if he is responsible to give you a full recital of the information you missed.
- Never ask questions or contribute to class, even when urged to by your teachers. It's far safer to be silent than to risk being considered a teacher's pet.
- Complain when teachers provide extra learning opportunities. They don't really want you to learn more, they just want to make college miserable for you.
- Do not read assignments before class. You can waste a lot of class time by asking questions about things that are explained in the textbook. Assume a look of pained confusion whenever the teacher refers to a point made in the text.
- Always ask teachers for references when you are given a library assignment. It is especially important that this be done before you look for the references yourself, or you will be putting yourself in the dangerous position of having to learn to use the library.
- Always try to be an exception to the rule. Avoid taking tests with the rest of the class. Assume that teachers will give you make-up tests or accept late papers, regardless of your reasons for missing the original tests or deadlines.

- Disagree with teachers in a haughty and condescending manner. This will show your fellow students that you are actually smarter than your teachers.
- Call assignments you do not understand "boring, irrelevant, or busy work." This a great way to insult your teachers and will also allow you to judge academic material before you comprehend it.
- Be a classroom lawyer. Always try to get what you want by twisting rules to your own advantage. "You never told us we had to capitalize the first words of the sentences in our papers!" "You said that we could miss a test if we had an emergency. Don't you think the death of my gerbil was an emergency?"
- Never do any more than is minimally required in a class. Only geeks and brown-nosers do more than they absolutely have to in order to pass a course.
- Never help to plan or participate in departmental or campus activities. Make it very clear that, for you, college consists of simply accumulating enough credit hours to graduate as quickly as possible with the minimum effort.
- Avoid using a teacher's office hours or making appointments. Show up when he is frantically finishing a lecture and explain that you must see him immediately.
- Wait until the last minute to pre-register or don't pre-register at all. Always expect your adviser to be available at your convenience and complain when the classes you want to take are closed. Try to find your adviser in his office during lunch or when you know he is in class; then tell the Dean or Registrar that you have been unable to pre-register because you have been looking for your adviser for three weeks and he is never in his office. When you meet with your adviser, be sure you have no idea of what classes you need or want to take. Put a pained expression on your face whenever he suggests a class that will help you overcome one of your academic weaknesses (e.g., math, writing, or speech).

CHAPTER 3

GETTING A JOB

Education is a valuable experience in and of itself, but for most of us, employment is the ultimate goal. Whether you are looking for your first job, right after college, or your tenth, many of the same rules apply.

EMPLOYMENT OPPORTUNITIES

A simple response to the question, "What can I do with a major in psychology?" might be, "just about anything that involves working with people." Another approach would be to list all of the occupations that psychology majors have successfully pursued. Neither of these approaches by itself, however, helps YOU to make career decisions. The purpose of this section is not only to provide you with some information about potential employment opportunities after completing your psychology degree, but also to make some suggestions about how to handle occupational decisions and successfully land that first job.

Let us begin with some important facts. The undergraduate major in psychology is a liberal arts degree, not a professional degree. It does not make you a psychologist or a professional counselor. These occupations require specific training at the graduate level and are regulated by state law. If such occupations interest you, be prepared to continue your education in graduate school.

While many occupations in psychology require graduate training, there are also many interesting and rewarding career opportunities available to individuals with a bachelors degree in psychology. Surveys of employers and psychology graduates indicate that the jobs obtained by psychology majors with a bachelors degree are most often in social service and business settings. Examples (from Zeller, 1988) of occupations available to psychology majors with a bachelors degree are listed below:

activity director • addiction counselor • administrative program assistant • admissions market analyst • admissions public relations director • admissions recruiter • admissions representative • adolescent care technician • adolescent chemical dependency counselor • advertising trainee • adviser-educator • affirmative action officer • agency representative • airline reservations clerk • alcohol counselor • alcoholism unit manager • area administrator • arena and sports facility instructor • assistant residence manager • assistant youth coordinator • association manager • behavior analyst • camp staff director caretaker • case tracking specialist • case worker • center supervisor • chemical dependency advocate • chemical dependency coordinator • chemical dependency counselor • chemical dependency secretary • chemical dependency technician • child care counselor • child care worker • child development worker • child protection worker • circulation manager • collection assistant • collector • college admissions representative • community activist • community correctional service worker • community outreach coordinator • community organizer • community service coordinator • community worker • compliance officer • consultant • cottage treatment team • counselor • counselor aid • counselor/therapist • county personnel officer • crime prevention coordinator • customer relations • customer service trainee • daily living aid • day-care aid • demonstration coordinator • deputy juvenile probation officer • developmental reading instructor • development officer • director of activity and recreation • director of alumni relations • director of day-care center • director of displaced homemakers • director of human services • director of education • director of planned parenthood • director of planning director of security • director of youth service bureau • driving instructor • drug counselor • early childhood specialist • education prevention specialist • education daytime coordinator • educational coordinator • educational representative • educational salesperson • educational textbook representative • employee assistance program specialist • employment counselor • employment representative • executive director • export order coordinator • field representative • foster home parent • grants coordinator • group home coordinator • group home counselor • group home parents • group leader • group worker • head of alumni affairs • head of fund raising • host/hostess • houseparent • human relations director • human services technician • infant stimulation teacher • information specialist • information referral specialist • inservice director • instructor • instructor-handicapped adult program • insurance agent • interviewer • investigator • juvenile justice planner • juvenile prevention program coordinator • juvenile specialist • living unit assistant • loading dock superintendent • management trainee • marketing manager • mental retardation professional • mental retardation unit manager • neighborhood outreach worker • occupational information developer • park and recreation director • patient service representative • personnel analyst • personnel coordinator • personnel generalist • planner-assistant • planner-evaluator • private school representative • private tutor • probation officer • program consultant • program coordinator • program director • project learning instructor • police training coordinator • public information officer • rehabilitation aid • relief houseparent • research analyst/planner • research assistant • research trainee • residence counselor • resident aid • resident caretaker • residential assistant • residential director • residential service coordinator • residential supervisor • resource developer • retail manager • salesperson • secretary • security officer • service advisor • social service director • social services supervisor • social studies teacher • social worker • social worker coordinator • statistical assistant • student activities adviser • supervisor • support service manager • task force coordinator • temporary admissions clerk • textbook coordinator • trainer • trainer-coordinator • veteran's adviser • volunteer coordinator • work activity program director • youth worker

As you can see, the possibilities are virtually endless—and this isn't even a complete listing. The jobs listed above are all opportunities available with only a bachelors degree.

A report from the National Science Foundation (1986) on employed bachelors-level graduates in psychology revealed that the following percentages were employed in five major areas one year after graduation.

50% → Business and industry

27% → Science and engineering

15% → Educational institutions

10% → Nonprofit organizations

8% → Federal, state, or local government

The work that these graduates performed in these various areas included the following broad range of areas, skills, and responsibilities.

30% → Management and administration

28% → Sales and professional services

16% → Teaching

12% → Production and inspection

14% → Other

These data clearly demonstrate that students who graduate with a psychology major are versatile individuals capable of gaining and maintaining meaningful employment in many different career areas.

JOB SKILLS POSSESSED BY PSYCHOLOGY MAJORS

"When people consider the question, 'What am I able to do with a bachelors degree in psychology,' they are usually thinking about what kind of job they might get. But there is another way of looking at this question that you should consider as part of your career planning. That is, you should seriously think about what in fact you are able to do in terms of the skills you may have acquired while majoring in psychology" (Edwards, 1989, p. 1)

Human Services Skills. These are skills necessary for successful employment in situations where direct services are provided to individuals who are in need of help.

- Perform institutional research and evaluation.
- Write reports and proposals clearly and objectively.
- Organize and lead groups, organizations, and committees.
- Recognize and understand behavioral and emotional disorders.
- Select, administer, score, and interpret psychological tests.
- Respond in an unbiased and tolerant way to individual differences.
- Display fundamental counseling skills with individual and groups.
- Collect, record, and report statistical and qualitative information.
- Perform crisis intervention techniques (e.g., listening and referral).
- Perform interviews to learn about people's history, problems, and plans.
- Contribute to program or treatment planning, evaluation, and implementation.
- Demonstrate small group skills (e.g., team building and conflict management).
- Communicate effectively and sensitively in both individual and group situations.
- Obtain information about problems through library research and personal contacts.
- Critically evaluate theories and research and apply the results to solve problems.
- Analyze problems on the basis of personal experience and psychological principles.
- Understand and modify your attitudes and actions in interactions with other people.

Research Skills. These are some of the types of skills essential to jobs in which information based on basic or applied research is provided to assist decision making.

- Construct and administer questionnaires.
- Use a variety of types of research equipment.
- Collect, organize, analyze, and interpret data.
- Present verbal presentations clearly and persuasively.
- Defend ideas in a clear, objective, nondogmatic manner.
- Be familiar with a variety of research methods and designs.
- Recruit research subjects and treat them in an ethical manner.
- Select, administer, score, and interpret various psychological tests.
- Write reports clearly, concisely, objectively, and in the correct style.
- Use library resources to research problems and prepare literature reviews.
- Identify problems and suggest solutions on the basis of research findings.
- Create easily understood graphs, tables, and verbal descriptions of results.
- Select and compute appropriate statistical tests and interpret their results.
- Assemble, interpret, and critically analyze research findings in specific areas.
- Use computers to write reports, analyze data, and perform bibliographic searches.
- Deal effectively with financial, temporal, and personnel constraints on research.

Students should realize that they may not develop these skills if they do not take full advantage of all their undergraduate opportunities (e.g., research and extracurricular activities). It is also equally important to obtain a broad, liberal education in addition to these specific skills. Because job markets are shifting constantly, it is crucial to avoid overspecialization and to strive for flexibility.

WHAT DO EMPLOYERS LOOK FOR IN A PSYCHOLOGY MAJOR?

The items in the three major categories of the following outline (taken directly from Edwards & Smith, 1988) are arranged in descending order of importance as rated by a large sample of employers from midwestern government, nonprofit, and commercial agencies, organizations, and companies that often hire undergraduate psychology majors. Psychology students are urged to take advantage of all their undergraduate opportunities to maximize the attainments of these skills, abilities, knowledge, and personal traits.

Skills and Abilities
- Writing proposals and reports
- Identifying and solving problems based on research and knowledge of behavior
- Conducting interviews
- Performing statistical analyses
- Designing and conducting research projects
- Performing job analyses
- Coding data
- Using computer programs to analyze data
- Systematically observing and recording behavior
- Constructing tests and questionnaires
- Administering standardized tests

Knowledge
- Formation and change of attitudes and opinions
- Principles and techniques of personnel selection
- How people think, solve problems, and process information
- Structure and dynamics of small groups
- Effects of the environment on people's feelings and actions
- Organizational development
- Principles of human learning and memory
- How people perceive and sense their environment
- Theories and research on organizational behavior, work, and productivity
- Theories and research on human development and stages of life
- Symptoms, causes, and treatments of abnormal behaviors

Personal Traits

- Ability to work with others in a team
- Motivation to work hard
- Positive attitude toward work and the organization
- Organization
- Leadership
- Maturity
- Flexibility
- Ability to communicate well
- Intelligence
- Problem-solving ability
- Integrity
- Tolerance for stress and ambiguity

MAKING DECISIONS ABOUT YOUR CAREER

An occupational choice can be one of the most difficult decisions a person makes, with consequences for both life style and life satisfaction. Unfortunately, many students approach this decision in a haphazard and informal manner; they neither explore potential occupations systematically nor prepare themselves adequately to successfully obtain a particular job. In fact, many students simply do not worry about careers until their senior year, when they discover that they lack courses or have failed to develop necessary skills for occupations that interest them.

Successful career planning requires careful and objective self-assessment, a realistic understanding of your aptitudes and skills, an awareness of responsibilities associated with potential employment settings, careful selection of experiences designed to develop marketable skills and knowledge, and an action plan for conducting a successful job search. Socrates said, "Know thyself." Two thousand years later, this is still good advice. It is essential that you know (or discover) your interests, preferences, values, aptitudes, and abilities. You can begin the process of self exploration by visiting your school's career services office. If your school does not offer such a service, start with the psychology department—they will be able to tell you where to go next. It's a good idea to start the process your freshman year—it's never too early to start to get familiar with the resources that are available to you.

An excellent resource for learning about various occupations is the **Occupational Outlook Handbook**, which is published every two years by the U.S. Department of Labor Statistics. This book is a comprehensive guide to occupations. It includes job descriptions, education and training requirements, advancement possibilities, salaries, and employment outlooks for 250 occupations. Go to the index at the back of the books and look up the page references for the occupations you are interested in pursuing. Note the titles of related jobs listed at the end of each occupational description, find these job titles in the index, and then read about them. Reading the Occupational Outlook Handbook can provide you with a wealth of information about a wide range of jobs in a short time with relatively little expenditure of effort.

You may also want to do some research on starting salaries for occupations that interest you. The Occupational Outlook Handbook has survey data on salaries organized by type of degree and occupation which is updated regularly. Listed below are the results of a 1994 salary survey. According to the September 1994 issue of *Salary Survey*, the average salary offered to bachelors-level psychology majors who graduated with the class of 1994 was $20,488 with a range from $16,249 to $32,500. (The average salary offered to those with a master's degree in psychology was $23,944 and a doctorate in psychology was $43,278.) The results of their survey for 30 functional employment areas are listed below in decreasing order of salary offer.

Functional Employment Area	Mean Salary Offer
Real Estate	$32,500
Chemicals and Allied Products	$32,000
Engineering / Surveying	$31,200
Consulting	$31,000
Metals and Metal Products	$28,000
Insurance	$27,750
Electrical and Electronics	$26,950
Research Organizations	$26,000
Widely Diversified	$25,400
Computer Software / Data Processing	$24,100
Protective Services	$24,000
Finance	$24,000
Federal Government	$23,689
Textiles and Apparel	$22,500
Hospitals	$22,025
Pharmaceuticals	$21,985
Computers and Business Equipment	$21,250
Transportation	$21,030
Merchandising	$20,945
Membership / Religious	$20,845
Building Materials and Construction	$20,709
Other Service Employers	$19,474
Health Services	$19,590
Local or State Government	$19,213

Education $18,028

Communication Services $17,333

Other Nonprofit Employers $17,233

Banking $16,967

Hospitality (Hotels and Restaurants) $16,614

Social Services $16,249

Developing Knowledge, Skills, and Characteristics

Part of knowing and marketing yourself involves a clear understanding of the specific knowledge, skills, and characteristics valued by employers and obtained through completing the bachelors degree in psychology. Numerous studies have documented the criteria that employers use when considering prospective employees, and they are summarized in the following lists. You can often gain the knowledge and skills in places where you would least expect it, and it is important to always consider who to apply the facts that you learn to real life situations. Psychology is, in many ways, a study of humanity and human nature, and this type of understanding can prove invaluable in the workplace. In the lists that follow, psychology courses that emphasize specific skills or types of knowledge are indicated in parentheses. Remember that it is not enough to develop these skills—you must learn to make them apparent to a prospective employer.

Knowledge
- How attitudes and opinions are formed and changed (Social Psychology)
- Principles and techniques of personnel selection and organizational development (Industrial Psychology)
- How people think, solve problems and process information (Cognitive Psychology)
- Structure and dynamics of small groups (Social Psychology)
- Effects of the environment on people's feelings and actions (Psychology of Motivation)
- Principles of human learning and memory (Psychology of Learning)
- Formation and change of attitudes and opinions
- Principles and techniques of personnel selection
- How people think, solve problems, and process information
- Structure and dynamics of small groups
- Effects of the environment on people's feelings and actions
- Organizational development
- Principles of human learning and memory
- How people perceive and sense their environment (Sensation and Perception)
- Theories and research on personality and individual differences (Theories of Personality)
- Principles of human needs and motivation (Psychology of Motivation)

- Theories and research on organizational behavior, work, and productivity (Industrial Psychology)
- Theories and research on human development and stages of life (Developmental Psychology)
- Symptoms, causes, and treatments of abnormal behaviors (Abnormal Psychology)

Skills
- Identifying and solving problems based upon a knowledge of research methodology and understanding of human behavior (General Psychology and Experimental Methods in Psychology)
- Performing statistical analyses (Statistics)
- Designing and conducting research projects (Experimental Psychology)
- Selecting, administering, and interpreting psychological tests (Tests and Measurement)
- Gathering and organizes information from multiple sources (Senior Seminar)
- Working productively as a member of a team (History and Systems of Psychology)
- Planning and carries out projects successfully (Independent Study)
- Ability to manage stress (Stress Management)
- Conducting interviews (Clinical Psychology)
- Writing proposals and reports (any psychology class that requires a paper)
- Speaking articulately and persuasively (any psychology class that requires an oral presentation)
- Performing job analyses (Industrial Psychology)
- Coding data (Statistics)
- Using computer programs to analyze data (Statistics)
- Systematically observing and recording behavior (Experimental Psychology)
- Constructing tests and questionnaires (Tests and Measurement)
- Recognizing and understanding behavioral and emotional disorders (Abnormal Psychology)
- Displaying fundamental counseling skills with individuals and groups (Counseling Psychology)
- Collecting, recording, and reporting statistical and qualitative information (Statistics)
- Using a variety of types of research equipment (Experimental Psychology)
- Organizing and leading groups, organizations, or committees
- Responding in an unbiased and tolerant way to individual differences
- Performing crisis intervention techniques (e.g., listening and referral) (Internship)
- Contributing to program or treatment planning, evaluation, and implementation
- Communicating effectively and sensitively in both individual and group situations
- Obtaining information about problems through library research and personal contacts
- Analyzing problems on the basis of personal experience and psychological principles
- Understanding and modifying your attitudes and actions in interactions with other people
- Presenting verbal presentations clearly and persuasively

- Defending ideas in a clear, objective, nondogmatic manner.
- Being familiar with a variety of research methods and designs.
- Recruiting research subjects and treat them in an ethical manner.
- Creating easily understood graphs, tables, and verbal descriptions of results.
- Dealing effectively with financial, temporal, and personnel constraints on research.

Characteristics
- Satisfactory grades
- Strong communication and interpersonal skills
- Outgoing personality
- Ability to present oneself in a positive manner
- Relevant previous employment
- Enthusiasm
- Flexibility
- Leadership
- Organization and problem solving abilities
- High energy level
- Maturity
- Ability to work with others in a team
- Motivation to work hard
- Positive attitude toward work and the organization
- Intelligence
- Problem-solving ability
- Integrity
- Tolerance for stress and ambiguity

It is, of course, more difficult to learn "characteristics" in a course, psychology or otherwise, but you would be surprised at how much control you really do have over your personality traits. When you have a specific goal in mind, you may find that you have a motivation to work on the shyness or disorganization that you once thought was "permanent."

Another important, yet often overlooked, aspect of skill and knowledge development is your selection of elective courses and a minor. For example, many graduates with a bachelor's degree in psychology are employed in business settings. Therefore, it would be wise to consider taking some business courses. Courses offered by other departments can be essential in obtaining job skills and knowledge for your future occupation as well. These courses can be used as electives or applied to a minor. Once you have narrowed down your potential employment settings, you should meet with your advisor to discuss the best selection of courses to help you obtain your career objective.

Potential employers also value some practical experience. There are several options to obtain this experience. One strategy is to seek part-time or full-time jobs related to your desired employment setting. Your school may also offer some type of co-op course, that combines an individual's on-site practical experience with individual meetings in which the practicum experience is discussed with the supervising faculty member. You may also want to consider volunteer activities that can provide practical experience in social service settings. Active involvement in leadership positions in student organizations (e.g., Psychology Club and Psi Chi) can also provide you with practical experience in developing, organizing, and running service programs.

But don't just take my word for it. Listen to some individuals who are in the positions that you would like to hold . . .

Advice from Employed Psychology Majors

- Don't wait until you are a senior to think about what you will put on your resume. Start this process when you are a freshman.

- Do things that will make it easy for people to write good letters of recommendation for you in the future.

- Don't be a loner. Develop a network of people who can help you to learn about and obtain the job you want.

- Try to personalize your education to fit your specific career goals.

- Develop specific career goals as early in your education as possible and then do everything you can to achieve these goals.

- Do some volunteer work or participate in a practicum, internship, or co-op program to gain experience and to make contacts.

- Develop interpersonal skills. If you are shy, do everything you can to overcome your shyness.

- Develop computer and statistical skills.

- Don't just learn things to pass tests. Learn things so that you can apply the knowledge that you learn in the job you want to obtain.

- Learn to become an articulate and persuasive writer and speaker.

- Get involved in extracurricular activities and assume leadership roles in these activities.

- Learn how to deal with stress and how to manage your time.

- Demonstrate to people that you are enthusiastic and motivated by actively seeking opportunities to become involved in activities that will broaden your experience and increase your network of people who can help you to increase your future career possibilities.

- Don't expect a good job to fall into your lap after graduation. Good jobs are a result of hard work, persistence, and planning.

- Realize that the world is full of people who are very different from you, and that you must learn to deal successfully with different kinds of people if you are to be successful.

ANOTHER SAMPLE SCHEDULE

As you have seen, a recurring piece of advice is to **plan ahead**. To help you do this, I have found another sample four-year plan (Hill, 1992); this time with the ultimate goal of getting a job.

FRESHMAN YEAR

- Schedule a meeting with your academic advisor to discuss your career interests and options. This meeting should not simply focus on what courses to take during the next semester.

- Begin to consider various careers. Investigate employment opportunities with a bachelors degree in psychology using resources available from your advisor and your career services office. Realize that some careers require graduate training either at the entry level or for eventual advancement.

- Begin a self-assessment process focusing on your interests, strengths, skills, and values. How well do they match your preliminary career goals?

SOPHOMORE YEAR

- Complete your self-assessment process. Compile a list of your interests, strengths (academic and personal), skills, and knowledge. Use this list to help focus your career choice.

- Continue the process of narrowing down your specific interests in the field of psychology and consider the type of employment you wish. Use the results of your self-assessment and on-campus resources to identify career options. You should focus your career choice by the end of your sophomore year so that you have time to take the appropriate preparatory coursework. *(continued)*

- Finish up the majority of your general education requirements, and begin to work your way through more of your psychology requirements.

- Meet with your academic advisor to discuss your progress toward degree completion and your career plans and options. You should discuss upper level course offerings in psychology that will best prepare you for your career.

- Begin to prepare a resume.

JUNIOR YEAR

- Re-evaluate your career choice. Are you still on the right track?

- Make plans to obtain relevant experience outside the classroom before the end of your senior year (e.g., volunteer work, co-op in Psychology, or a directed study involving independent research).

- Meet with your academic advisor to discuss your progress toward degree completion and your career plans and options. Review your course selections for the major field in psychology and your minor, if you have one.

- Contact people in the profession you are seeking to enter, and conduct some information interviews to learn more about career options.

SUMMER BETWEEN JUNIOR AND SENIOR YEAR

- Use the summer months to build your job information network, prepare a polished resume, and continue to refine your career aspirations.

SENIOR YEAR

- Meet with your academic advisor during fall semester to discuss your progress toward degree completion and your career plans and options. Review your course selections for the major field in psychology and your minor, if you have one.

- Obtain a copy of your transcript from the Registrar and review it carefully for any errors.

- Identify three individuals (e.g., faculty members and past employers) who are willing and able to write STRONG letters of recommendations for you.

- Review your resume. Ask faculty members to review your resume.

- Practice for interviews with the psychology faculty. The initial interview can be one of the most critical hurdles in getting a job, so be as prepared as possible.

THE JOB SEARCH

By the beginning of your senior year, you should have decided on a career path and obtained the basic skills and knowledge necessary for an entry position in that field. Unfortunately, your future employers will not seek you out; you will have to aggressively seek out and convince them that **you** are the employee that they should hire. To accomplish this you must first identify position openings and make contacts. Once you make these contacts, you must be able to present yourself in such a way as to convince these contacts that you are the person for the job. With an effective resume and good interview skills, you will be able to put your best foot forward and be well on your way to getting a job (Portions of this section come from Ware, 1953).

Identifying Potential Job Openings

Your career services office is, of course, the most logical place to begin your job search. There are, however, many other resources that you should take advantage of. Ask people you know to identify individuals with whom you might talk to about your career interest. Friends, family, past or present employers, and people with whom you have done volunteer work are all excellent resources for contacts.

The newspaper is also a good source for information regarding potential employment. Every day, jobs are listed under countless headings, including administrative assistant, customer service, sales, day care, and management—all of which are potential career options with your psychology degree. Read the job descriptions in advertisements very carefully, or you may miss a good potential opportunity. When you find an advertisement that sounds promising, send a cover letter and resume to the provided contact name. We will discuss the resume and cover letter later in this chapter.

Another strategy is to use the yellow pages of the phone book to identify companies, agencies or organizations that may employ people in your career interest area. You should call these organizations and ask for the name of the person in the position that interests you. Ask to speak to that person. When you contact him or her, explain that you are an undergraduate student approaching graduation and that you are interested in obtaining a job in their profession. Ask if they would be available to meet with you for an "information interview" to discuss their profession. The worst that can happen is that they will say "no." Be prepared to offer them several potential meeting times. Do not attempt to conduct the interview on the phone at that moment. The person may be busy and only able to give you cursory information. Be sure you go to the interview with a list of well thought-out questions. Toward the end of the information interview, ask if they can suggest other people to talk to about the profession. This will help to expand your contacts.

Your Resume

The word "resume" is derived from the French word for summary and it is just that—a summary of your career objectives, educational history, and work experience. A resume should answer two important questions for a potential employer: **"What can you do for me?"** (answered in your career objectives) and **"Why should you be considered for this job?"** (answered in your sections on educational history and work experience). Irish (1978) states that job seekers must be able to answer the following three question to write effective resumes: Who am I? What do I do well? What do I want?

Your resume is a critical element of an effective job search. It is the single most effective piece of direct mail that you can send, providing a sort of "you-at-a-glance." If you research job leads in person, always leave a resume with the human resources person as a kind of calling card. Potential employers will ALWAYS expect to receive a resume, whether or not they specifically request it, whenever you apply for a job through the mail. Remember, before an employer meets you in person, your resume is the only impression they have of you.

If you are going to interview for a job, be sure that you bring an extra copy of your resume with you. It will come in handy if you need to fill out an application, for much of the information that you need will be there in front of you. When you begin an interview, the resume smoothes over the introductions—the interviewer already knows a few things about you and has an easy jumping-off point from which to start the conversation.

Your resume is your chance to emphasize the things about you that you think are important, an opportunity to highlight your real strengths. If the interviewer has your resume in front of him or her, the conversation will likely turn to things that you feel confident discussing. After the interview, your resume is the only record the employer has after the interview. Remember—an effective resume is neat, easily read, and provides a concise summary of your professional expectations, education, and experience, and nothing says that you can't develop more than one resume—tailored to different occupational goals.

Now that you see how important a resume is, you may feel intimidated about developing your own. **DON'T.** If you have never written a resume before, it may seem unnatural to write about yourself. Keep in mind that you are not bragging in a resume—you are simply attempting to give a person who does not know you a realistic idea of what you are like and what you can do. If you keep your goals and objectives in the front of your mind as you embark on the resume writing process, you will be fine. Who knows, you may even discover that you enjoy writing about yourself!

Your resume should be written to clearly communicate the message that you possess valuable skills, not that you have simply existed for the past 21 years. One way to do this is to include action verbs that describe what you have accomplished (e.g., "I **designed** and **administered** a student satisfaction survey, **analyzed** the results with a microcomputer statistics program, and **presented** my findings at an undergraduate research conference). The following list of verbs (modified from Lock, 1988) is a good place to start your search for strong words to describe what you have accomplished.

Adapted	Designed	Investigated	Protected
Advised	Developed	Judged	Questioned
Administered	Diagnosed	Learned	Read
Analyzed	Directed	Lectured	Reasoned
Applied	Discovered	Led	Recommended
Approved	Displayed	Listened	Reconciled
Arranged	Drew	Located	Recorded
Assembled	Edited	Maintained	Recruited
Assessed	Encouraged	Managed	Reduced
Assisted	Estimated	Measured	Reinforced
Balanced	Established	Mediated	Reorganized
Budgeted	Evaluated	Memorized	Repaired
Classified	Expedited	Mentored	Reported
Clarified	Followed	Monitored	Researched
Coached	Forged	Motivated	Restored
Collected	Formulated	Nurtured	Reviewed
Communicated	Gathered	Observed	Revised
Compared	Generated	Operated	Scheduled
Compiled	Guided	Organized	Shaped
Completed	Handled	Originated	Simplified
Computed	Helped	Participated	Solved
Conceived	Identified	Perceived	Spoke
Conceptualized	Implemented	Performed	Synthesized
Conducted	Improved	Persisted	Streamlined
Confronted	Improvised	Persuaded	Studied
Constructed	Increased	Planned	Supervised
Contrasted	Influenced	Prepared	Supported
Controlled	Initiated	Presented	Taught
Coordinated	Integrated	Processed	Tested
Comprehended	Inspired	Produced	Trained
Counseled	Installed	Programmed	Treated
Created	Instructed	Promoted	Tutored
Decided	Interpreted	Proposed	Validated
Defined	Interviewed	Proved	Volunteered
Demonstrated	Invented	Provided	Wrote

If one of these words is close to something that you have done but does not quite describe it, look it up in a thesaurus and check its list of synonyms for the right word. Another good source for action verbs is the list of objectives that appear on class syllabi. These objectives contain the skills you will acquire as a result of successfully completing these classes.

Sample Resumes. The following are two sample resumes. Keep in mind that these are just two examples of success—there are countless winning combinations of skills and experience. Just be confident and put your best foot forward and you are sure to find a job that matches your needs.

MICHELLE A. POYNTER

Marian College
3200 Cold Springs Road
Indianapolis, Indiana 46222
(317) 929-0145

Objectives: Short-term : Experience working with mentally or physically handicapped people
Long-term : Graduate education resulting in a mental health career

Education: Sophomore psychology major at Marian College with a GPA of 3.28 on a 4.0 scale.

Relevant Classes: General Psychology, Statistical Methods, Abnormal Psychology, Developmental Psychology, Experimental Psychology I, Introduction to Computers, Introduction to Speech, English Composition

Experience: May to September, 1988
Angola Community Sheltered Workshop (Angola, IN)
Responsible for training and supervising mentally and physically handicapped persons in a
     factory atmosphere and assisting supervisors with daily job assembly and quality control.

May to September, 1988
Sutton's Super Value (Hamilton, IN)
Responsible for price and merchandise information input, daily receipts, and customer service.

May to September, 1987
Subway Sub Shop (Angola, IN)
Responsible for food preparation, maintenance, financial transactions, record-keeping.

January to September, 1986 and 1987
CTN Data (Hamilton, IN)
Responsible for physical upkeep of an eight room office complex.

May 1987 to Present
Youth for Christ / Campus Life (Great Lakes Region)
Responsible for supervising high school students on trips to Florida and Washington D.C. and
     organizing meetings in the Northeast Indiana area.

January 1989 to Present
Student Administrator of the Psychology Department's Big Psyb / Little Psyb Program
Responsible for coordinating all functions of the program.

Activities: Marian College Booster Club (1988 to present)
Booster Club Fund Raising Committee (1988 to present)
Intramural Softball and Volleyball (1987 and 1988)
Psychology Club (1987 to present)
Convocation Committee (1988 to present)
Campus Life / Youth for Christ (1983 to 1987)
Freshman Orientation Leader (1988 to present)
Big Psyb to incoming freshman Psychology majors (1988 to present)

References: Available upon request

MATTHEW V. LaGRANGE

Marian College
3200 Cold Springs Road
Indianapolis, Indiana 46222
(317)929-0145

Objectives:	Educational: To earn a Ph.D. in clinical psychology.
	Career: To teach and perform research in a university setting.
Education:	Bachelor of Art, Marian College (expected June, 1989)
	Major: Psychology Minor: Computer Applications
	Cumulative GPA (4-point scale) = 3.78
	GPA in Psychology = 3.80
	GPA in Computer Applications = 4.00
	GRE scores (verbal = 540, math = 700)
Honors	Elected to Psi Chi
	Dean's List (each semester since spring 1986)
	President of the Student Body
	Vice President of the Student Body
	Secretary of the Student Body
	Student member of the American Psychological Association
Organizations:	Member of the Psychology Club
	Member of the Judicial Panel
	Member of the Conduct Appeals Panel
Research:	LaGrange, M., & Appleby, D. C. (1987, April). *Effects of mood on time perception*. Paper presented at Mid-America Undergraduate Research Conference, Evansville, IN.
	LaGrange, M. V., & Appleby, D. C. (1988, April). *Factors affecting academic honesty*. Paper presented at Mid-America Undergraduate Research Conference, Evansville, IN.
	Fohl, M. M., Koebel, J. M., LaGrange, M. V., & Webb, P. M. (1988, April*). A student-produced evaluation form of teaching effectiveness*. Paper presented at Mid-America Undergraduate Research Conference, Evansville, IN.
	LaGrange, M. V., & Appleby, D. C. (1989, April*). Student and faculty perception of academic dishonesty as a function of learning or grade orientation*. Paper presented at Mid-America Undergraduate Psychology Research Conference, Evansville, IN.
	LaGrange, M. V., & Appleby, D. C. (manuscript submitted). *Factors that affect academic dishonesty in college students*. College Teaching.
Experience:	Served as research assistant for Dr. Drew Appleby (1987-89).
	Residential Supervisor at the Center for Neuropsychological Rehabilitation (1988 - 1989)
	Counselor at the St. Vincents Hospital Stress Center (1989)

References: Dr. Drew Appleby
Marian College
3200 Cold Spring Road
Indianapolis, IN 46222

Dr. Paul Riley
St. Vincents Hospital
8700 Harcourt Road
Indianapolis, IN 46268

Dr. Joseph Hingtgen
Marian College
3200 Cold Spring Road
Indianapolis, IN 46222

Dr. Lance Trexler
Center for Neurological Rehabilitation
9621 North Meridian
Indianapolis, IN 46209

As you know, no matter how good your resume is, you can't send it anywhere without some sort of introduction. That introduction comes most often in the form of a cover letter. The cover letter should be succinct and to the point, but should tell the reader who you are and what you are looking for. The following is an example of an acceptable cover letter that will accompany a resume to a potential employer. Be absolutely sure your letter is as professional-looking as possible. Use a laser printer to produce it, and be absolutely sure that it contains no spelling, grammatical, capitalization, or punctuation errors. These types of errors will doom your application process from the very beginning.

A Sample Cover Letter

December 10, 1994

Mr. Gerald Harshman
Director of Personnel
Phillips Research Company
3756 Morehouse Drive
Indianapolis, IN 46224

Dear Mr. Harshman,

I am interested in applying for the research statistician position that was advertised in the January 8 issue of the Indianapolis Star. As indicated by my resume, I will receive a B.A. degree in psychology from Marian College in May, 1995. I believe that my background and experience in statistics and research qualify me for this challenging type of work.

I would be most happy to meet with you at your convenience to further describe my qualifications for and interest in this position. Letters of recommendation are available from the references listed in my resume.

Please contact me at: Marian College
                          3200 Cold Spring Road
                          Indianapolis, IN 46222-1997
                          317-929-0456

Thank you for your attention.

Sincerely,

Tim Ellinger

Your Job Interview

Your interview with a prospective employer is your opportunity to impress him or her with your potential as a future employee. The job interview is the forum where almost all hiring decisions are made—your "make or break" opportunity. Although few initial interviews result in an immediate job offer, the first interview plays a crucial role in identifying candidates that the company may look at more closely. Therefore, it is critical that you make a strong, favorable first impression. The most important personal qualities that employers look for are good communication skills, clearly defined professional goals, and an honest, outgoing personality.

Take interviews very seriously and prepare for each one in advance. If possible, try to make an appointment with one of the psychology faculty or another cooperative professional to do a video-taped practice interview. In addition, be knowledgeable about the employer with whom you are interviewing. This will enable you to ask specific questions about the company that will generate a favorable impression. Finally, follow up the interview with a thank-you note. This reinforces the favorable impression you made during the interview and keeps you fresh in the interviewer's mind.

Types Of Interviews. Although no two interviews are identical, there are several typical forms of interviews:
- **Patterned Interview** - Such interviews are highly structured, systematic and designed to serve as a stable yardstick against which applicants can be measured. They are specially adapted for research and designed to overcome problems of inconsistency. Essentially, the identical questions are asked of all applicants, and then the individual responses are compared. The typical use of a patterned interview is in initial screening of many applicants to weed out the more obviously unqualified. Most on-campus interviews follow this format.
- **Non-Directive or Free-Association Interview** - Typically employs open-ended type questions such as "Tell me about yourself." This allows applicants to express themselves in their own unique way and offers greater exposure to an applicant's personality and attitudes. However, the interviewer needs considerable skill to keep applicants from rambling, and to objectively analyze data. Many campus interviewers will *appear* to follow this format.
- **Stress Interview** - The purpose of this method is to measure the applicant's ability to handle stressful situations. Stress interviews are used to weed out individuals who react defensively or get easily injured. Stress interviews are seldom used on-campus.
- **Group and/or Area Interview** - Group interviews are often used for higher-level business and academic positions. Typically a "search committee" composed of personnel representatives, managers, and often psychologists will examine an applicant. Each interviewer will often be assigned a particular area of the applicant's background on which to concentrate (e.g., experience, education, or family background). This approach can be

exhausting for the applicant, especially if the interviewing is structured on a one-on-one basis, or if it takes several hours or days.

Preparation for the Interview. Research the organization before interviewing. Know the size of the firm, its potential growth, its competition, and its prospects for the future. Consult company and other literature, such as *Standard & Poor's, The Wall Street Journal, Business Week*, etc. for this information. You should also know the locations of its major offices/plants and its reputation within the industry. Knowledge of this information insures a more productive interview because the company representative will be able to spend less time describing the company and more time interviewing you.

The interviewer is going to ask you a number of probing questions (see sample questions). Prepare for them by first attempting to predict what will be asked and then by practicing your answers. Role play with someone who knows you well. If possible, record the session. Examine your responses and evaluate your performance. You should try to express yourself in a clear and logical manner, and to communicate a sense of self-confidence and direction. The best way to practice for interviews is in a video-taped mock interview. This method is excellent for providing feedback regarding your responses, mannerisms, and overall interviewing style.

Dress Appropriately. A good first impression in the interview is essential. Some studies have indicated that physical appearance is the one strongest and most consistent predictor of recruiting success, even ranking over such factors as grades and work experience! With that in mind, you must maximize your physical appearance to compete effectively. Although there are exceptions, you'll rarely go wrong if your dress conservatively. For **women**, this means a classic navy blue or gray suit, with a modest updated blouse. Although a tailored dress can also be worn, a business suit is considered the "uniform" for interviewing. A pair of classic medium-heeled pumps, with a neutral stocking will compliment the look. Accessories and makeup are fine, as long as they are understated. *Keep it simple*. Cologne and perfume should be used sparingly. Hair should be clean, neatly styled, and away from face. For **men**, again, conservative is the rule of thumb. This means a navy blue or gray suit, with a white long-sleeved shirt that has been professionally laundered. A tie that is understated and coordinated will add to the professional image you want to portray. Shoes in black, brown, or cordovan that are polished will certainly complete the look. Jewelry for men should be limited to a wedding ring or class ring. Men also must be careful not to overdo the cologne or aftershave. Hair, along with sideburns and mustaches should be neatly trimmed. Beards are risky, and probably should not be worn. Of course, these guidelines are just GENERAL rules—there are plenty of settings where a suit would be considered too formal. If possible, try to find out how the individuals in the positions and companies in question typically dress You can assess this by browsing through company literature, or better yet, actually observing the employees at the company. If the company is close, drop by during lunch or as people are leaving at the end of the day. This will give you some idea of what would be considered appropriate dress.

During the Interview. In the vast majority of cases, students are rejected because of one major flaw—lack of proper career planning. Even if you view the company as nothing more than a career experiment, don't make vague statements such as, "I'll take most any job" or "I want to work with people." In your research you should have identified typical starting assignments—apply for those positions. If you perform well, opportunities for greater mobility will appear after your initial assignment.

Recruiters' Objectives. You can increase your employment chances if you keep in mind the recruiters' objectives. Recruiters have specific entry level vacancies to fill. They want people who are seriously interested in a career in a particular field. They need answers to the following questions: Why does this person want to work for my company?
For what position would this individual be best suited? What are the qualifications of the interviewee? How does he or she compare with his or her peers? If you are prepared to answer these questions, you can save the recruiter a lot of work and probably land the job.

Nervousness. Recruiters are aware that job interviewing can cause extreme nervousness. Usually a recruiter will make allowance for this, especially if it is one of the applicant's first interviews. Try not to fidget with your hands or articles of clothing. Keep frequent eye contact with the interviewer, but don't stare. In most instances, nervousness will become less of a factor after two or three interviews. For this reasons, it is wise to save your most important interviews until you have acquired some practice. Above all, don't become discouraged; interviewing is a learned skill.

Eye Contact. Having good eye contact is very important when communicating, especially when interviewing or meeting a prospective employer. Lack of direct eye contact can give a person the wrong impression about you. We typically think that a person who cannot look us in the eye may either be shy, hiding something, or dishonest. Maintain good eye contact when communicating; it will leave others with a positive impression of you.

Body Language. We can say many things with our bodies using nonverbal communication. Make sure that your body language portrays a message of friendliness and openness. When communicating, watch out for folded hand and arms, crossed legs, head in a downward position, or not sitting directly facing the person with whom you are talking. These gestures could lead others to think you are either very closed, aloof, or distant.

Be Candid. While subterfuge may get you the job, it isn't likely to keep it for you. The hiring of an employee is, after all, an agreement to buy what the employee has to sell. Unless both parties form an honest evaluation of each other, the sale is apt to be canceled.

Enthusiasm. Your interviewer has probably worked for his or her company for several years. The organization provides a recruiter with a good income, security, and an interesting career; in other words he or she is dedicated to the company. The interviewer expects you to have similar feelings or to at least exhibit enthusiasm for a potential position with the firm. A well-researched presentation is probably the best way to demonstrate this quality. Make your questions reflect your knowledge of the employer. Find out about the normal routine of the position in which you are interested, where you can expect to be in five years, and opportunities for further professional education. The idea is to convey a sense of long term interest. Above all, don't be too concerned bout salary, fringe benefits, or retirement plans. Convey your enthusiasm for the work, not for the awards.

Think on Your Feet. Don't let the interviewing situation stampede your confidence. Make sure you get the opportunity to express your strong points fully. Your answers should be factual, sincere, but should not convey conceit. You should be able to point out improvement trends in your grade point average if it appears low. Be sure to call attention, without bragging, to any supervisory or leadership positions you may have held, even volunteer positions (most internships can legitimately be described as experience, so be sure to emphasize them). Make sure the recruiter is aware of the percentage of your college expenses which you have earned (Most employers appreciate the difficulties involved in working while attending college, and will made due allowances for a lower grade point average or fewer extracurricular activities.)

After the Interview, Thanks. Send a short personal note to the interviewer, and anyone else you have spoken to regarding employment. This can be an extremely effective reinforcer. Although this step is often recommended, few applicants follow up on the suggestion. Thus, you can underscore your uniqueness just by this simple act of courtesy.

Tips For Thank-You Letters
- Express your appreciation for the interviewer's time and consideration.
- Indicate your interest in the position.
- Reemphasize your strengths and qualifications.
- Mention something you didn't say during the interview (e.g., work experience or accomplishments).
- Enclose a resume to refresh the interviewer's memory.
- Unless the recruiter has indicated otherwise, state that you will contact him/her on a specific date to follow-up.
- Be proactive; call as you said you would!

Twenty Questions Frequently Asked During Interviews
- Tell me about yourself. Expand on your resume.
- For what position are you applying?
- What are your long-term career goals? Where would you like to be in ten years?
- Why do you feel that you will be successful in...?
- What supervisory or leadership roles have you held?
- How do you spend your spare time?
- What have been your most satisfying and most disappointing experiences?
- What are your strongest (weakest) personal qualities?
- Give me some examples that support your stated interest in...
- Why did you select to interview with us?
- What courses did you like best? Least? Why?
- What did you learn or gain from your part-time and summer job experiences?
- Which geographic location do you prefer? Why?
- Would you prefer on-the-job training or a formal program?
- What can you do for us now? What can I do for you?
- What are your plans for graduate study?
- Why did you choose your major?
- Why are your grades low?
- Tell me about your extracurricular activities and interests.
- Why did you quit your various jobs?

Common Interviewee Questions
(Questions are pertinent only if the answer influences you)
- How much travel is normally expected?
- Do employees normally work many hours of overtime?
- Can I progress at my own pace or is it structured?
- How frequently do you relocate professional employees?
- What is the average age of your first-level supervisors?
- Is the sales growth in the new product line sustainable?
- How much contact and exposure to management is there?
- At what level is an employee placed in the "exempt" status?
- Is it possible to move through the training program faster?
- When does the training program begin? Only in June?
- What is the housing market like in your city?
- How much freedom is given to and discipline required of the new people?
- Does the firm recommend any night courses the first year?
- How often are performance reviews given?
- Is it possible to transfer from one division to another?

- How much decision-making authority is given after one year?
- Have any new product lines been announced recently?
- How soon after graduation would I expect to report for work?
- How much input does the new person have on geographical location?
- In your firm, is this position more analytical or more people-oriented?
- In promotions, are employees ever transferred between functional fields?
- Does the firm provide employee discounts?
- Is a car provided to traveling personnel?
- Is the city difficult to adjust to compared to this campus community?
- What is the average age of top management?
- What is the normal routine of a ... like?
- How much independence is allowed in dress and appearance?
- Is public transportation adequate?
- What is the average time to get to ... level in the career path?

WARNING: The initial interview is <u>not</u> the time to inquire about salary!

Fifteen Knockout Factors
(Reasons why candidates are rejected)
- Lack of proper career planning - purposes and goals defined - needs direction.
- Lack of knowledge of field of specialization - not well qualified - lacks depth.
- Inability to express thoughts clearly and concisely - rambles.
- Insufficient evidence of achievement or capacity to excite action in others.
- Not prepared for the interview - no research on company - no presentation.
- No real interest in the organization or the industry - merely shopping around.
- Narrow location interest - unwilling to relocate later - inflexible.
- Little interest and enthusiasm - indifferent - bland personality.
- Overbearing - overaggressive - conceited - cocky - aloof - assuming.
- Interested only in best dollar offer - too money conscious.
- Asks no or poor questions about the job - little depth and meaning to questions.
- Unwilling to start at the bottom - expects too much too soon - unrealistic.
- Makes excuses - evasive - hedges on unfavorable factors in record.
- No confidence and poise - fails to look interviewer in the eye - immature.
- Poor personal appearance - sloppy dress - dress lacks sophistication

Job Fairs

At this point I would like to say a word or two about job fairs. Though they may not be available to everyone, they can provide valuable contacts, so if you're lucky enough to have one in your area, check it out!

Job fairs are a great way to see a range of recruiters hiring for sciences, social services, computers, writers, and managers all in one place. Job fairs provide you with the chance to meet with recruiters who might otherwise have been inaccessible. In order to make the most of the opportunities they provide, prepare ahead with the following strategy.

Before the Fair
- **Clarify your goals for the job fair.** Expect to initiate contact with recruiters to learn more about jobs and companies that interest you. Don't expect them to seek you out, and don't expect any job offers to be made to you at the job fair. Companies that are interested in you will contact you for later on-site interviews.
- **Review a list of companies that will be attending.** Identify those you plan to talk with and read their literature and any other information you can find. Don't rule out a company just because you haven't heard of them; at the moment, smaller companies are often more likely to hire than the Fortune 500's.
- **Prepare a list of at least four questions for each organization based on your research.** Appropriate questions reveal both information about you and demonstrate your knowledge of the company. For example, "I have read about your new drive toward sales at every level and believe my summer experience in cold calling will help me to be effective with you organization. What have the practical difficulties of implementing this initiative been?" Avoid questions about salary and benefits at initial interviews.
- **Prepare a one minute commercial about yourself to introduce yourself to all companies you plan to contact.** Give your name, school, and major. Clearly state your career goals. List ten tasks the job requires on the left side of a sheet of paper; list the ways you have done similar tasks on the right side; then explain the similarities. Demonstrate your knowledge of and interest in the organization. Be open, honest, enthusiastic, and concise, and practice, practice, practice.
- **Prepare a one page resume without a career objective.** The second page of a two-page resume is often torn off and thrown away by job fair coordinators.

At the Fair
- **Greet employers with a firm handshake and make eye contact.** Avoid distracting mannerisms or gestures.
- **Give them a copy of you resume.**
- **Give your one minute commercial.** Make it clear why they would benefit from hiring you (i.e., connect your background to their needs); then state your interest in them. Be

prepared to discuss anything mentioned on your resume, answering all questions concisely. Ask them your prepared questions, but allow them to direct the flow of the conversation.

- **Request a business card of each employer with whom you speak.**

After the Fair

- **Write prompt follow-up letters to employers you are interested in pursuing.** Thank them, reaffirm your interest, remind them of your strengths, and clarify any points you feel you mishandled or left incomplete.

(This is a modified version of an article entitled "Preparing for a Job Fair" that appeared in <u>Career Currents</u>, the career planning and placement newsletter of Hanover College.)

CHAPTER 4

ETHICS AND PSYCHOLOGY

Certain ethical codes govern the pursuit of psychological knowledge, both professionally and educationally. Though they may be intangible, moral factors in psychology should always be the first priority.

A PREAMBLE TO ETHICAL PRINCIPLES OF PSYCHOLOGISTS

Psychologists have an ethical code (Ethical Principles of Psychologists, APA, 1992) and a book for the interpretation and application of the code in specific situations (Casebook of Ethical Principles of Psychologists, APA, 1974). This code specifies the manner in which scientific research is conducted and services to clients are rendered. The preamble to this code is presented below to familiarize students with the nature of this publication.

Psychologists work to develop a valid and reliable body of scientific knowledge based on research. They may apply that knowledge to human behavior in a variety of contexts. In doing so, they perform many roles, such as researcher, educator, diagnostician, therapist, supervisor, consultant, administrator, social interventionist, and expert witness. Their goal is to broaden knowledge of behavior and, where appropriate, to apply it pragmatically to improve the condition of both the individual and society. Psychologists respect the central importance of freedom of inquiry and expression in research, teaching, and publication. They also strive to help the public in developing informed judgments and choices concerning human behavior. This Ethics Code provides a common set of values upon which psychologists build their professional and scientific work.

This code is intended to provide both the general principles and the decision rules to cover most situations encountered by psychologists. It has as its primary goal the welfare and protection of the individuals and groups with whom psychologists work. It is the individual responsibility of each psychologist to aspire to the highest possible standards of conduct. Psychologists respect and protect human and civil rights, and do not knowingly participate in or condone unfair discriminatory practices.

The development of a dynamic set of ethical standards for a psychologist's work-related conduct requires a personal commitment to a lifelong effort to act ethically; to encourage ethical behavior by students, supervisees, employees, and colleagues, as appropriate; and to consult with others, as needed, concerning ethical problems. Each psychologist supplements, but does not violate, the Ethics Code's values and rules on the basis of guidance drawn from personal values, culture, and experience.

Inherent in the code are certain principles that each psychologist must hold dear. A psychologist, or anyone associated with psychological professions, must respect each individual's sense of self-worth and dignity, and must strive to understand the nuances of human nature. Psychologists are put in positions of power, in relation to their patients and to their human and animal research subjects. Under no circumstances should this power be abused. Listed below are some of the central tenets to the psychological professions, as quoted directly from Ethical Principles of Psychologists (APA, 1992).

Principle A: Competence

Psychologists strive to maintain high standards of competence in their work. They recognize the boundaries of their particular competencies and the limitations of their expertise. They provide only those services and use only those techniques for which they are qualified by education, training, or experience. Psychologists are cognizant of the fact that the competencies required in serving, teaching, and/or studying groups of people vary with the distinctive characteristics of those groups. In those areas in which recognized professional standards do not yet exist, psychologists exercise careful judgment and take appropriate precautions to protect the welfare of those with whom they work. They maintain knowledge of relevant scientific and professional information related to the services they render, and they recognize the need for ongoing education. Psychologists make appropriate use of scientific, professional, technical, and administrative resources.

Principle B: Integrity

Psychologists seek to promote integrity in the science, teaching, and practice of psychology. In these activities psychologists are honest, fair, and respectful of others. In describing or reporting their qualifications, services, products, fees, research, or teaching, they do not make statements that are false, misleading, or deceptive. Psychologists strive to be aware of their own belief systems, values, needs, and limitations and the effect of these on their work. To the extent feasible, they attempt to clarify for relevant parties the roles they are performing and to function appropriately in accordance with those roles. Psychologists avoid improper and potentially harmful dual relationships.

Principle C: Professional and Scientific Responsibility

Psychologists uphold professional standards of conduct, clarify their professional roles and obligations, accept appropriate responsibility for their behavior, and adapt their methods to the needs of different populations. Psychologists consult with, refer to, or cooperate with other professionals and institutions to the extent needed to serve the best interests of their patients, clients, or other recipients of their services. Psychologists' moral standards and conduct are personal matters to the same degree as is true for any other person, except as psychologists' conduct may compromise their professional responsibilities or reduce the public's trust in psychology and psychologists. Psychologists are concerned about the ethical compliance of their colleagues' scientific and professional conduct. When appropriate, they consult with colleagues in order to prevent or avoid unethical conduct.

Principle D: Respect for People's Rights and Dignity

Psychologists accord appropriate respect to the fundamental rights, dignity, and worth of all people. They respect the rights of individuals to privacy, confidentiality, self-determination, and autonomy, mindful that legal and other obligations may lead to inconsistency and conflict with the exercise of these rights. Psychologists are aware of cultural, individual, and role differences, including those due to age, gender race, ethnicity, national origin, religion, sexual orientation, disability, language, and socioeconomic status. Psychologists try to eliminate the effect on their work of biases based on those factors, and they do not knowingly participate in or condone unfair discriminatory practices.

Principle E: Concern for Others' Welfare

Psychologists seek to contribute to the welfare of those with whom they interact professionally. In their professional actions, psychologists weigh the welfare and rights of their patients or clients, students, supervisees, human research participants, and other affected persons, and the welfare of animal subjects of research. When conflicts occur among psychologists' obligations or concerns, they attempt to resolve these conflicts and to perform their roles in a responsible fashion that avoids or minimizes harm. Psychologist are sensitive to real and ascribed differences in power between themselves and others, and they do not exploit or mislead other people during or after professional relationships.

Principle F: Social Responsibility

Psychologists are aware of their professional and scientific responsibilities to the community and the society in which they work and live. They apply and make public their knowledge of psychology in order to contribute to human welfare. Psychologists are concerned about and work to mitigate the cause of human suffering. When undertaking research, they strive to advance human welfare and the science of psychology. Psychologists try to avoid misuse of their work. Psychologists comply with the law and encourage the development of law and social policy that serve the interests of their patients an clients and the public. They are encouraged to contribute a portion of their professional time for little or no personal advantage.

ETHICAL PRINCIPLES IN THE CONDUCT OF
RESEARCH WITH HUMAN PARTICIPANTS

There are certain very concrete rules that the field of psychology requires in the research and educational settings. Although the details may vary from institution to institution, the code of behavior is essentially the same.

The following general principle and its ten sub-principles are quoted directly from Ethical Principles in the Conduct of Research with Human Subjects (APA, 1982, p. 5-7). Copies of this publication are available in the psychology office and the college library.

The decision to undertake research rests upon a considered judgment by the individual psychologist about how best to contribute to psychological science and human welfare. Having made the decision to conduct research, the psychologist considers alternative directions in which research energies and resources might be invested. On the basis of this consideration, the psychologist carries out the investigation with respect and concern for the dignity and welfare of the people who participate and with cognizance of federal and state regulations and professional standards governing the conduct of research with human participants.

- In planning a study, the investigator has the responsibility to make a careful evaluation of its ethical acceptability. To the extent that the weighing of scientific and human values suggests a compromise of any principle, the investigator incurs a correspondingly serious obligation to seek ethical advice and to observe stringent safeguards to protect the rights of human participants.

- Considering whether a participant in a planned study will be a "subject at risk" or a "subject at minimal risk," according to recognized standards, is of primary ethical concern to the investigator.

- The investigator always retains the responsibility for ensuring ethical practice in research. The investigator is also responsible for the ethical treatment of research participants by collaborators, assistants, students, and employees, all of whom, however, incur similar obligations.

- Except in minimal-risk research, the investigator establishes a clear and fair agreement with research participants, prior to their participation, that clarifies the obligations and responsibilities of each. The investigator has the obligation to honor all promises and commitments included in that agreement. The investigator informs the participants of all aspects of the research that might reasonably be expected to influence willingness to participate and explains all other aspects of the research about which the participants inquire. Failure to make full disclosure prior to obtaining informed consent requires additional safeguards to protect the welfare and dignity of the research participants. Research with children or with participants who have impairments that would limit understanding and/or communication requires special safeguarding procedures.

- Methodological requirements of a study may make the use of concealment or deception necessary. Before conducting such a study, the investigator has a special responsibility to (a) determine whether the use of such techniques is justified by the study's prospective scientific, educational, or applied value; (b) determine whether alternative procedures are available that do not use concealment or deception; and (c) ensure that the participants are provided with sufficient explanation as soon as possible.

- The investigator respects the individual's freedom to decline to participate in or to withdraw from the research at any time. The obligation to protect this freedom requires careful thought and consideration when the investigator is in a position of authority or influence over the participant. Such positions of authority include, but are not limited to, situations in which research participation is required as part of employment or in which the participant is a student, client, or employee of the investigator.

- The investigator protects the participant from physical and mental discomfort, harm, and danger that may arise from research procedures. If risks of such consequence exist, the investigator informs the participant to that fact. Research procedures likely to cause serious or lasting harm to a participant are not used unless the failure to use these procedures might expose the participant to risk of greater harm, or unless the research has great potential benefit and fully informed and voluntary consent is obtained from each participant. The participant should be informed of procedures for contacting the investigator within a reasonable time period following participation should stress, potential harm, or related questions or concerns arise.

- After the data are collected, the investigator provides the participant with information about the nature of the study and attempts to remove any misconceptions that may have arisen. Where scientific or humane values justify delaying or withholding this information, the investigator incurs a special responsibility to monitor the research and to ensure that there are no damaging consequences for the participant.

- Where research procedures result in undesirable consequences for the individual participant, the investigator has the responsibility to detect and remove or correct these consequences, including long-term effects.

- Information obtained about a research participant during the course of an investigation is confidential unless otherwise agreed upon in advance. When the possibility exists that others may obtain access to such information, this possibility, together with the plans for protecting confidentiality, is explained to the participant as part of the procedure for obtaining informed consent.

THE CARE AND USE OF ANIMALS IN RESEARCH

The Principle E from Ethical Principles of Psychologists (APA, 1992) deals with the care and use of animals in research.

An investigator of animal behavior strives to advance understanding of basic behavioral principles and/or to contribute to the improvement of human health and welfare. In seeking these ends, the investigator ensures the welfare of animals and treats them humanely. Laws and regulations notwithstanding, an animal's immediate protection depends upon the scientist's own conscience.

- The acquisition, care, use, and disposal of all animals are in compliance with current federal, state or provincial, and local laws and regulations.

- A psychologist trained in research methods and experienced in the care of laboratory animals closely supervises all procedures involving animals and is responsible for ensuring appropriate considerations of their comfort, health, and humane treatment.

- Psychologists ensure that all individuals using animals under their supervision receive explicit instruction in experimental methods and in the care, maintenance, and handling of the species used. Responsibilities and activities of individuals participating in a research project are consistent with their competencies.

- Psychologists make every effort to minimize discomfort, illness, and pain of animals. A procedure subjecting animals to pain, stress, or privation is used only when an alternative procedure is unavailable and the goal is justified by its prospective scientific, educational, or applied value. Surgical procedures are performed under appropriate anesthesia; techniques to avoid infection and minimize pain are followed during and after surgery.

- When it is appropriate that the animal's life be terminated, it is done rapidly and painlessly.

THE RIGHTS AND RESPONSIBILITIES OF RESEARCH PARTICIPANTS

Students performing psychological research have an ethical obligation to (a) respect the rights of their research participants (i.e., subjects) and to (b) communicate their responsibilities to them. The following outline (taken directly from Korn, 1989) describes these rights and responsibilities of research participants.

The Rights of Research Participants

- Participants should know the general purpose of the study and what they will be expected to do. Beyond this, they should be told everything a reasonable person would want to know in order to decide whether to participate.

- Participants have the right to withdraw from a study at any time after beginning participation in the research. A participant who chooses to withdraw has the right to receive whatever benefits were promised.

- Participants should expect to receive benefits that outweigh the costs or risks involved. To achieve the educational benefit, participants have the right to ask questions and to receive clear, honest answers. When participants do not receive what was promised, they have the right to remove their data from the study.

- Participants have the right to expect that anything done or said during their participation in a study will remain anonymous and confidential, unless they specifically agree to give up this right.

- Participants have the right to decline to participate in any study and may not be coerced into research. When learning about research is a course requirement, an equivalent alternative to participation should be available.

- Participants have a right to know when they have been deceived in a study and why the deception was used. If the deception seems unreasonable, participants have the right to withhold their data.

- When any of these rights is violated or participants object to anything about a study, they have the right and the responsibility to inform the appropriate university officials, including the chairman of the psychology department.

The Responsibilities of Research Participants

- Participants have the responsibility to listen carefully to the experimenter and ask questions in order to understand the research.

- Be on time for the research appointment.

- Participants should take the research seriously and cooperate with the experimenter.

- When the study has been completed, participants share the responsibility for understanding what happened.

- Participants have the responsibility for honoring the researcher's request that they not discuss the study with anyone else who might be a participant.

ACADEMIC INTEGRITY

The search for truth, the transmission of knowledge, and the facilitation of moral development are the goals of higher education. These goals cannot be achieved unless the men and women who participate in their achievement are honorable persons with a common desire for the highest level of academic integrity. Education is a personal endeavor, and much of the moral checks must come from within. For this reason, many schools require that you sign a pledge stating that your work is yours alone. Violations of this type of pledge are listed below.

Cheating: Using or attempting to use unauthorized materials or information to gain an unfair advantage over other students in any academic exercise. This includes using crib notes during an exam, copying answers from another student's paper during an exam, and receiving information between exams in multiple sections of a course.

Multiple Submission: Submitting the same assignment in two or more courses without obtaining prior permission of both instructors. This includes submitting the same or essentially the same term paper, speech, or computer program in two classes without obtaining both instructors' permission.

Fabrication: Falsifying or inventing information in any academic exercise. This is of especial application to lab courses, in reporting false data in a laboratory assignment. It also applies to written work, however, such as padding a bibliography with references not cited in the text.

Misuse of Materials: Abusing or unauthorized removing of academic materials from the library or any other campus location. This includes removing pages from a book or magazine in the library or taking a book from the library without checking it out.

Misrepresentation: Presenting false excuses or using deception to receive a higher grade or to avoid fulfilling the requirements of an assignment or course. It also includes inventing a false excuse to miss a test or obtaining unauthorized help from another student on a take-home exam.

Facilitation of Academic Dishonesty: Helping another student to violate any provision of code, by allowing another student to copy from your paper during an exam, informing another student of the contents of an exam before he/she takes it, writing a paper for another student who then submits it for course credit, or transmitting a false excuse for another student to a faculty member.

Plagiarism: Representing the words or ideas of another as one's own in any academic exercise. It goes beyond the scope of other academic offenses and is considered a criminal offense—it is theft of intellectual property—and can lead to fines or even imprisonment. Plagiarism has many variations, and it is possible to be guilty of plagiarizing without even knowing it. The guidelines below should help you learn to recognize potential plagiarizing. Remember, it is better to be safe than sorry, and when in doubt, cite your source!

Forms of Plagiarism

- "The use of another's writing without proper use of quotation marks. Do not, under any circumstances, copy onto your paper a direct quotation without providing quotation marks and without crediting the source" (Lester, p. 47).
- "The borrowing of a word or phrase, the use of an idea, or the paraphrasing of material if that phrase, idea, or material is not properly introduced and documented. Also included in this category of plagiarism is the mere rearrangement of phrases from the original into a new pattern" (Lester, p. 47).
- It is also plagiarism to "take, buy, or receive a paper written by someone else and present it as your own" (Corder and Ruszkiewicz, p. 633).
- A form of academic dishonesty related to plagiarism is collusion, defined as "collaboration with someone else in producing work you claim to be entirely your own" (Corder and Ruszkiewicz, p. 633).

Ways to Avoid Plagiarism

- "Acknowledge borrowed material within the text by introducing the quotation or paraphrase with the name of the authority from whom it was taken.
- Enclose within quotation marks all quoted materials, even single words and phrases.
- Make certain that paraphrased material is written in your own style and language. The simple rearrangement of sentence patterns is unacceptable.
- Provide a bibliographic entry for every book or magazine that appears in a written work" (Lester, p. 47).
- Be certain that all written work you submit is your own. You may (and in some cases should) ask others to review your work, but "any changes, deletions, rearrangements, or corrections should be your own work" (Corder and Ruszkiewicz, p. 633).

Plagiarists may receive penalties from the legal system, but most academic violators are disciplined within the school community. Academic penalties are normally determined by the instructor of the class and the department chairperson. Some cases may require action by higher ranking college officials or the school-wide disciplinary organization. This type of action can result in serious disciplinary sanctions including suspension or expulsion from the school.

IN CONCLUSION

The world of psychology is a large and exciting one, with an infinite number of possibilities and opportunities. Each one of you will experience a slightly different part of that world, and the pieces that you choose will help to determine the path to your future. As a parting word I can only advise you always to ASK. Never be afraid to seek help when you need it, to question your professors and advisors when you don't understand something. When you enter the world after college, question the way things are—if they don't seem right or true, try to find another answer.

In this handbook, I have tried to give you some of the answers, some of the proven "facts of life" of the psychology world. If this book has helped you to feel more comfortable and confident as you pursue your studies and post-graduate life, I will feel that I have succeeded in my mission.

Best of luck!

CHAPTER 5

RESOURCES

PUBLICATIONS ON CAREERS IN PSYCHOLOGY

The following publications contain information about careers in the general field of psychology and its specialty areas. The best introduction to these topics is a booklet entitled <u>Careers in Psychology</u> (the source of this list of publications) that is available free of charge to students from the American Psychological Association at the address give below.

American Association of State Psychology Boards. (Updated). <u>Entry requirements for professional practice of psychology: A guide for students and faculty</u>. New York: Author. (Available from the Office of Professional Affairs, APA, 1200 17th Street, NW, Washington, DC 20036)

American Psychological Association. (Rev. biannually). <u>Graduate study in psychology and associated fields</u>. Washington, DC: Author. (Address: American Psychological Association, 1200 17th Street, NW, Washington, DC 20036)

American Psychological Association. (1983). <u>Psychology as a health care profession</u>. Washington, DC: Author. (See address above.)

American Psychological Association, Division of Consulting Psychology. (1980). <u>Consulting psychology</u>. Washington, DC: Author. (Available from APA Division of Consulting Psychology, 631 A Street, SE, Washington, DC 20036)

American Psychological Association, Division of Consumer Psychology. (Updated). <u>Careers in consumer psychology</u>. Washington, DC: Author. (See address above.)

American Psychological Association, Division of Military Psychology. (Updated). <u>Military psychology: An overview</u>. Washington, DC: Author. (See address above.)

American Psychological Association, Division of Industrial and Organizational Psychology. (Updated). <u>A career in industrial-organizational psychology</u>. Washington, DC: Author. (See address above.)

American Psychological Association, Division of School Psychology. (Updated). <u>The school psychologist</u>. Washington, DC: Author. (See address above.)

Careers, Inc. (1982). <u>Psychologist, school</u>. Largo, FL: Author. (Cost: $1.00. Address: P.O. Box 135, Largo, FL 34294-0135.)

Careers, Inc. (1982). <u>Psychologist, clinical</u>. Largo, FL: Author. (Cost: $1.00. See address above.)

Careers, Inc. (1982). <u>Counselor, school</u>. Largo, FL: Author. (Cost: $1.00. See address above.)

Careers, Inc. (1982). <u>Psychologist</u>. Largo, FL: Author. (Cost: $1.25. See address above.)

Catalyst National Headquarters. (1975). <u>Psychology</u>. (Career Opportunities Series No. C-19). New York: Author. (Address: 14 East 60th Street, New York, NY 10022)

Catalyst National Headquarters. (1975). <u>Psychology</u>. (Educational Opportunities Series No. E-19). New York: Author. (See address above.)

Chronicle Guidance Publications. (1982). <u>Psychologists</u>. (Occupational brief No. 144). Moravia, NY: Author. (Address: P.O. Box 1190, Moravia, NY 13118-1190)

Fretz, B. R., & Stang, D. J. (1988). <u>Preparing for graduate study: Not for seniors only!</u> Washington, DC: American Psychological Association. (See address above.)

Rudman, J. (1980). <u>Psychologist</u> (Career Examination Series No. C-627). Syosset, NY: National Learning Corp. (Address: 212 Michael Drive, Syosset, NY 11791)

Super, D. E., & Super, C. M. (1982). <u>Opportunities in psychology</u> (4th ed.). Skokie, IL: National Textbook. (Address: 4255 Touhy Avenue, Lincoln, IL 60646)

Woods, P. J. (Ed.). (1979). <u>The psychology major: Training and employment strategies</u>. Washington, DC: American Psychological Association. (See address above.)

ORGANIZATIONS

The American Psychological Association (APA) is a professional society of more than 70,000 teachers, researchers, professionals, and students that advances psychology as an academic discipline, a science, and a means of promoting human welfare. APA publishes scholarly journals, holds an annual convention, and concerns itself with the social and ethical responsibilities of professional psychologists. Student membership in APA is encouraged, and membership application forms can be obtained in the psychology office.

Psi Chi is the national honor society for students majoring or minoring in psychology who meet the following criteria.

1. Completed a minimum of 9 hours of psychology courses.

2. Maintained a 3.25 GPA in psychology courses.

3. Maintained a 3.00 overall GPA.

RELATED HANDBOOKS

Handbooks are comprehensive sources of information written by leading psychological experts who periodically summarize the information in their fields of specialization. According to Reed and Baxter (1983): "Most handbooks have several characteristics that make them especially well suited for narrowing a topic and beginning a literature search. They provide an authoritative summary of a particular area, including evaluations of theory and research. They are written by experts in the field. Although one person sometimes writes a handbook, more commonly one person edits the contributions of many authors, each of whom writes in his or her special area of interest and expertise. They are usually written at a level for a beginning graduate student in the particular subfield and are more comprehensive than most textbooks. They contain extensive reference lists" (p. 23-24).

The following is a partial list of handbooks that are in print.

Theories of Psychology
Abnormal Psychology
Psychological Assessment
Experimental Psychology
Motivation
Personality Theory and Research

Projective Techniques
Child Psychology
Child Development

The Annual Review of Psychology is written each year by experts in various fields of psychological specialization. It contains chapters that summarize the current research and predict the future trends in these areas.

PSYCHOLOGICAL JOURNALS

Although psychologists and psychology students use books, handbooks, and annual reviews, their primary source of information for research and scholarly activity is journals. The following is a partial list of the available journals in the area of psychology and related fields.

Abnormal Psychology
Addictive Behavior
Aggressive Behavior
American Journal of Community Psychology
American Journal of Psychiatry
American Journal of Psychology
American Psychologist
American Scientist
Animal Behavior
Animal Learning and Behavior
Annual Review of Rehabilitation
APA Monitor
Applied Psychological Measurement
Behavior Modification
Behavior Research Methods, Instruments, and Computers
Behavior Therapy
Behavioral and Brain Sciences
Behavioral Neuroscience
Behavioral Science
Biological Psychology
British Journal of Psychology
Bulletin of the Psychonomic Society
Canadian Journal of Psychology
Child Development
Cognitive Psychology
Cognitive Therapy and Research
Contemporary Psychology
Counseling Psychologist

Counselor Education and Supervision
Developmental Psychobiology
Developmental Psychology
Educational and Psychological Measurement
Educational and Psychological Testing
Environment and Behavior
Exceptional Children
Genetic Psychology
Group and Organizational Studies
Human Factors
Human Relations
Intelligence
International Journal of Intercultural Relations
International Journal of Psychoanalytic Psychotherapy
International Review of Applied Psychology
Journal of Abnormal and Social Psychology
Journal of Abnormal Psychology
Journal of Applied Behavior Analysis
Journal of Applied Behavior
Journal of Applied Behavioral Science
Journal of Applied Psychology
Journal of Applied Rehabilitation Counseling
Journal of Applied Social Psychology
Journal of Behavior Therapy and Experimental Psychology
Journal of Clinical Psychology
Journal of Community Psychology
Journal of Comparative and Physiological Psychology
Journal of Comparative Psychology
Journal of Consulting and Clinical Psychology
Journal of Consulting Psychology
Journal of Consumer Research
Journal of Counseling and Development
Journal of Counseling Psychology
Journal of Cross-Cultural Psychology
Journal of Educational Psychology
Journal of Experimental Child Psychology
Journal of Experimental Psychology
Journal of Experimental Psychology: Animal Behavior Processes
Journal of Experimental Psychology: General
Journal of Experimental Psychology: Human Learning and Memory
Journal of Experimental Psychology: Human Perception and Performance
Journal of Experimental Psychology: Learning, Memory, and Cognition
Journal of Experimental Social Psychology

Journal of General Psychology
Journal of Genetic
Journal of Heredity
Journal of Higher Education
Journal of Humanistic Psychology
Journal of Memory and Language
Journal of Neurophysiology
Journal of Occupational Psychology
Journal of Personality
Journal of Personality and Social Psychology
Journal of Psychology
Journal of Rehabilitation
Journal of Research in Personality
Journal of Safety Research
Journal of School Psychology
Journal of Social Issues
Journal of Social Psychology
Journal of the Experimental Analysis of Behavior
Journal of Verbal Learning and Verbal Behavior
Journal of Vocational Behavior
Learning and Motivation
Marriage and Family Living
Memory and Cognition
Memory and Cognition
Merrill-Palmer Quarterly of Behavior and Development
Organizational Behavior and Human Decision Process
Organizational Behavior and Human Performance
Organizational Dynamics
Perception
Perception and Psychophysics
Perceptual and Motor Skills
Personality and Social Psychology Bulletin
Personnel and Guidance Journal
Personnel Journal
Personnel Psychology
Physiological Psychology
Physiology and Behavior
Professional Psychology
Professional Psychology: Research and Practice
Psychological Abstracts
Psychological Bulletin
Psychological Documents
Psychological Issues

Psychological Record
Psychological Reports
Psychological Review
Psychology in the Schools
Psychology in Women Quarterly
Psychology Today
Psychophysiology
Psychotherapy
Psychotherapy Theory, Research and Practice
Public Opinion Quarterly
Public Personnel Management
Rehabilitation Counseling Bulletin
Rehabilitation Literature
Rehabilitation Record
Representative Research in Social Psychology
School Counselor
Small Group Behavior
Social Forces
Social Problems
Social Psychology
Social Psychology Quarter
Sociology of Work and Occupations
Sociometry: A Journal of Research in Social Psychology
Teaching of Psychology
Vocational Guidance Quarterly
Work and Occupations

Bibliography

American Psychological Association. (1986). <u>Careers in psychology</u>. Washington, DC: Author.

American Psychological Association. (1987). <u>Casebook on ethical principles of psychologists</u>. Washington, DC: Author.

American Psychological Association. (1982). <u>Ethical principles in the conduct of research with human participants</u>. Washington, DC: Author.

American Psychological Association. (1992). <u>Ethical principles of psychologists</u>. Washington, DC: Author.

American Psychological Association. (Revised biannually). <u>Graduate study in psychology and associated fields</u>. Washington, DC: Author.

Benner, R. S., & Hitchcock, T. C. (1986). <u>Life after liberal arts</u>. Charlottesville: University of Virginia.

Bloom, L. J., & Bell, P. A. (1979). Making it in graduate school: Some reflections about the superstars. <u>Teaching of Psychology, 6</u>, 231-332.

Bloomquist, D. W. (1981). <u>A guide to preparing a psychology student handbook</u>. Washington, DC: American Psychological Association.

Career Placement Council. (1989, September). <u>Salary Survey</u>. Bethlehem, PA: Author.

Corder, J. W., & Ruszkiewicz, J. J. (1985). <u>Handbook of current English</u>. Glenview, IL: Scott, Foresman.

Descutner, C. J., & Thelen, M. H. (1989). Graduate student and faculty perspectives about graduate school. <u>Teaching of Psychology, 16</u>, 58-60.

Edwards, J. (1989). <u>What are you able to do with a bachelor's degree in psychology?</u> Unpublished manuscript, Loyola University, Chicago.

Fretz, B. R., & Stang, D. J. (1988). <u>Preparing for graduate study in psychology: Not for seniors only!</u> Washington, DC: American Psychological Association.

Herbstrith, J., Mauer, B., & Appleby, D. C. (1990, April). Applicant characteristics valued by graduate programs in psychology. Paper presented at the Mid-America Undergraduate Psychology Research Conference, Indianapolis.

Hill, G. W. (1992) Kennesaw State College Psychology Department Handbook. Available through the Kennesaw State College Psychology Department, Marietta, GA, 30061.

Irish, R. K. (1978). Go hire yourself an employer. Garden City, NY: Anchor Press / Doubleday.

Johnson, C. S. (1989). Mentoring programs. In M. L. Upcroft & J. N. Gardner (Eds.), The freshman year experience: Helping students survive and succeed in college (pp. 118-128). San Francisco: Jossey-Bass.

Johnson, D. E. (1988). Psychology major handbook. John Brown University, Siloam Springs, AK.

Kibler, W. L., Nuss, E. M., Paterson, B. G., & Pavela, G. (1988). Academic integrity and student development. Washington, DC: College Administration Publications.

Korn, J. H. (1988). Students' roles, responsibilities, and rights as research participants. Teaching of Psychology, 15, 74-78.

Lester, J. D. (1967). Writing research papers: A complete guide. Glenview, IL: Scott, Foresman.

Lester, V., & Johnson, C. S. (1981). The learning dialogue: Mentoring. In J. Fried (Ed.), Education for student development. San Francisco: Jossey-Bass.

Lock, R. D. (1988). Job search: Career planning guidebook, book II. Pacific Grove, CA: Brooks/Cole.

Lunneborg, P. W., & Wilson, V. M. (1982). Job satisfaction in different occupational areas among psychology baccalaureates. Teaching of Psychology, 12, 21-22.

National Science Foundation. (1986). Characteristics of recent science/engineering graduates: 1984. Washington, DC: Author.

Milton, O., Pollio, H., & Eison, J. (1986). Making sense of college grades. San Francisco: Jossey-Bass.

Newman, J. H. (1947). The idea of a university. New York: Longmans Green. (Original work published 1852).

Pion, G., & Bramblett, P. (1985). Salaries in psychology 1985: Report on the 1985 APA salary survey. Washington, DC: Author.

Reed, J. G., & Baxter, P. M. (1983). Library use: A handbook for psychology. Washington, DC: American Psychological Association.

Shandley, T. C. (1989). The use of mentors for leadership development. NASPA Journal, 21(1), 59-66.

Steininger, M., Newell, J. D., & Garcia, L. T. (1984). Ethical issues in psychology. Homewood, IL: Dorsey Press.

Walter, T. and Siebert, A. (1993) Student Success: How to succeed in college and still have time for your friends. Fort Worth, TX: Holt, Rinehart, & Winston, Inc.

Ware, M. (1993). Career development and opportunities for psychology majors. Pamphlet available form Dr. Mark Ware, Psychology Department, Creighton University, Omaha, NE, 68178.

Wise, P. S. (1988). Psychology, your major, and you. In P. J. Woods (Ed.), Is psychology for them?: A guide to undergraduate advising. (pp. 9-13). Washington, DC: American Psychological Association.

Woods, P. J. (Ed.) with Wilkerson, C. (1987). Is psychology the major for you? Washington, DC: American Psychological Association

Zeller, M. J. (1988). Titles of jobs in human services for students with a bachelor's degree in psychology. In P. J. Woods (Ed.), Is psychology for them?: A guide to undergraduate advising. (pp. 195-196). Washington, DC: American Psychological Association.